BEGINNING FINGERSTYLE ARRANGING

AND TECHNIQUE FOR GUITAR

A SUPPLEMENT TO

The Complete Fingerstyle Guitar Method

PATRICK JOHNSON

Alfred, the leader in educational publishing,
and the National Guitar Workshop,
one of America's finest guitar schools, have joined
forces to bring you the best, most progressive
educational tools possible. We hope you will enjoy
this book and encourage you to look for
other fine products from Alfred and the
National Guitar Workshop.

ISBN 0-7390-3674-2 (Book & CD)

*This book was acquired, edited and produced
by Workshop Arts, Inc., the publishing arm of
the National Guitar Workshop.
Nathaniel Gunod, managing and acquisitions editor
Burgess Speed, editor
Ante Gelo, music typesetter
Timothy Phelps, interior design
CD recorded at Exodus Studio, Mississauga, Ontario, Canada.
Photographs on page 9 by Larry Lytle.
All other interior photographs by Stella Jurgen, 17 Designs, Mississauga, Ontario, Canada, unless otherwise noted.*

Cover photographs by Karen Miller.

TABLE OF CONTENTS

ABOUT THE AUTHOR

PHOTO • KRISTA CAMERON

Pat Johnson began teaching guitar in 1995. He joined the faculty of the National Guitar Workshop in 1999 and teaches songwriting, fingerstyle guitar, slide guitar and other courses at its Connecticut campus. His regular performances in Easter, Ontario have helped him to develop a growing audience. In 2003 he released his debut CD, *Pat Johnson's Songs from the Town Boredom Built.* He resides in the village of Charleston Lake, Ontario, Canada. You can visit Pat online at www.patjohnson.ca.

"This guitar-based instrumental track is a joy to listen to. The relaxing melodies and its bluesy feel fit perfectly when you're watching the snow fall on a crisp winter day. Johnson plays the slide guitar like the lost art that it is. Ever so carefully, yet forceful at times. This track is among the highlights of his record, 'Songs from the Town Boredom Built.' "

> Gregory Joseph on Pat Johnson's "Cottage Slide" (Instrumental Song of the Year)
> 2 Walls Webzine

"Pat Johnson knows a thing or two about style. The blues loving singer-songwriter from Brockville, ON has crafted an admiral debut...clean finger-style guitar gives the bluesier material a Mississippi John Hurt sort of charm and his lyrics are humorous and entertaining. [He] would surely make even Taj Mahal crack a smile."

> Brent Hagerman
> Exclaim!

DEDICATION

This book is dedicated to my first guitar teacher, Mr. Richard Crotty. I hope this book will make you proud.

ACKNOWLEDGEMENTS

Thanks to Nathaniel Gunod, Bob Farmer, the folks at Mr. C's Gift of Music, Al Torrance, Lois Crotty, the folks at NGW, Chris DeZordo, Mom & Dad, Krista Cameron, M&M Cameron and my many students.

INTRODUCTION

The objective of this book is to help you develop the skills needed to create arrangements of music where a melody can be self-accompanied on the guitar, creating the illusion of two or more guitars. Throughout the book, melodies—some familiar and some original—will be used to build a series of arrangements using various techniques useful to the up-and-coming arranger. Some melodies are arranged several times to demonstrate how an arrangement can be developed, from simple to more complex.

This book assumes that you have some basic guitar skills, such as playing 1st position chord shapes and simple fingerpicking patterns. Examples appear in both standard music notation and tablature (TAB), so you need not be an experienced music reader to use this method. It is highly recommended, however, that you supplement this book with a sight-reading method such as *Sight-Reading for the Contemporary Guitarist* by Tom Dempsey (National Guitar Workshop/Alfred #21954). A brief explanation of standard music notation is included in this book to get you started reading if you are interested. It is not difficult to do, and will reap many rewards.

The focus will be on melody and how to support it using fingerstyle techniques. Take your time with this material, practice regularly, and you will be creating and playing fingerstyle guitar arrangements before you know it.

Have fun!

00

Track 1

A compact disc is available with this book. Using the disc will help make learning more enjoyable and the information more meaningful. Listening to the CD will help you correctly interpret the rhythms and feel of each example. The symbol on the left appears next to each song or example that is performed on the CD. The track number below each symbol corresponds directly to the song or example you want to hear. Example numbers are above the symbol. Track 1 will help you tune to this CD.

CHAPTER 1

Getting Started

TUNING

Learning to tune your guitar is your first responsibility. If your instrument is out of tune, the music you make will not amount to much. Check your tuning before every practice session. Depending on how long you practice, you may want to check your tuning intermittently during your session. Bending strings and aggressive playing will tend to put a guitar out of tune.

The many methods used to tune the guitar can be grouped into two categories: using your ears, and using an electronic tuner. Even if you use an electronic tuner, your ears should be the final test.

ELECTRONIC TUNERS

Electronic tuners come in two categories: *guitar tuners* and *chromatic tuners*. Guitar tuners are designed to tune the guitar to *standard tuning* (E–A–D–G–B–E). Chromatic tuners will tune your guitar strings to any of the 12 tones. This is useful for experimenting with *alternate tunings* (tunings where one or more strings are changed from standard tuning), which are used later in this book. Electronic tuners come with built-in microphones that can hear your acoustic guitar, or you can plug in an electric guitar. It is recommended that, even if you opt to use an electronic tuner, you should always double-check the tuning with your ears.

USING YOUR EARS—RELATIVE TUNING

In this method we will tune the guitar strings relative to one another. You will need a reference *tone* (musical sound) to get started. You can get this from a tuning fork, pitch pipe, another guitar or a piano.

1. Match the open 6th string (low E—the string closest to your chin when the guitar is placed in proper playing position, see page 14) to your reference tone (E).
2. Match the open 5th string (A) to the A on the 5th fret of the 6th string.
3. Match the open 4th string (D) to the D on the 5th fret of the 5th string.
4. Match the open 3rd string (G) to the G on the 5th fret of the 4th string.
5. Match the open 2nd string (B) to the B on the 4th fret of the 3rd string.
6. Match the open 1st string (high E) to the E on the 5th fret of the 2nd string.

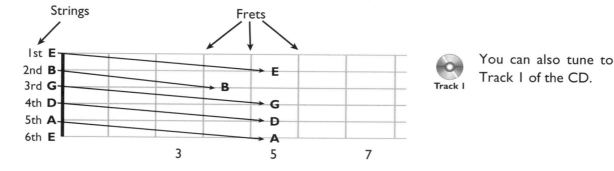

You can also tune to Track 1 of the CD.

Track 1

MUSICAL PITCHES AND THE FRETBOARD

THE MUSICAL ALPHABET

Every *pitch* (degree of highness or lowness of a tone) is given a letter name from the *musical alphabet,* which has seven letters that repeat: A–B–C–D–E–F–G, A–B–C etc. These seven pitches are the *natural* pitches.

By now, you have probably memorized the names of your strings. This is very important. To review, they are as follows:

6th (lowest-sounding) string = E   3rd string = G
5th string = A   2nd string = B
4th string = D   1st (highest-sounding) string = E

Our next step is to learn the names of the pitches on all of the strings at every fret.

HALF STEPS AND WHOLE STEPS

Pitches are arranged on the fretboard using *whole steps* and *half steps*. A whole step is a distance of two frets. For example, from the 1st fret to the 3rd fret is a whole step. A half step is a distance of one fret. For example, from the 2nd fret to the 3rd fret is a half step.

All natural pitches are a whole step apart with the exception of B to C and E to F, which are a half step apart. With this knowledge, we can identify all of the natural pitches on the fretboard.

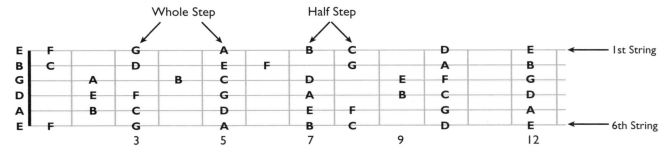

ACCIDENTALS

Notice on the diagram above that there are spaces between most of these natural pitches. *Accidental* symbols are used to name the pitches on these frets.

♯   *Sharp*. Raises a note one half step (one fret).

♭   *Flat*. Lowers a note one half step (one fret).

♮   *Natural*. Returns a note to its natural position.

As the illustration above shows, there is an F on the 1st fret of the 1st string and a G on the 3rd fret. The pitch on the 2nd fret is G♭ (G-flat) or F♯ (F-sharp). Every pitch named with an accidental can be called by a flat name or a sharp name. For example, G♭ and F♯ are the same pitch and are played on the same fret. These are called *enharmonic equivalents*.

READING TABLATURE

Tablature, or TAB, is a graphic way of writing music for the guitar. There are six lines, each representing one of the strings. Numbers placed on the lines indicate what fret to play on that string.

In this book, the tablature is written parallel to the standard music notation (see page 8). Tablature indicates only fret numbers and strings. For other information, such as how fast or slow to play the music, you must refer to the standard music notation.

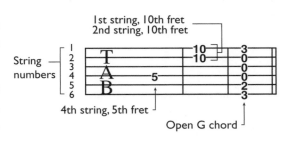

For purposes of communication, some knowledge of *standard music notation* and the most common terminology is needed. Nowadays, there are many books and magazines containing educational material and popular songs for guitarists. If you want to be able to read the arrangements and examples in the books, then this information is for you.

PITCH

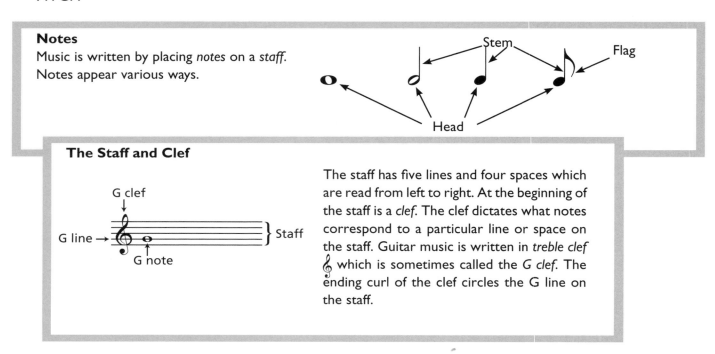

Notes

Music is written by placing *notes* on a *staff*. Notes appear various ways.

Stem

Flag

Head

The Staff and Clef

G clef

G line →

G note

Staff

The staff has five lines and four spaces which are read from left to right. At the beginning of the staff is a *clef*. The clef dictates what notes correspond to a particular line or space on the staff. Guitar music is written in *treble clef* which is sometimes called the *G clef*. The ending curl of the clef circles the G line on the staff.

Here are the notes on the staff using the G clef:

Notes on the lines:

Notes in the spaces:

E G B D F   D F A C E G

Ledger Lines

The higher a note appears on the staff, the higher it sounds. When a note is too high or too low to be written on the staff, *ledger lines* are used.

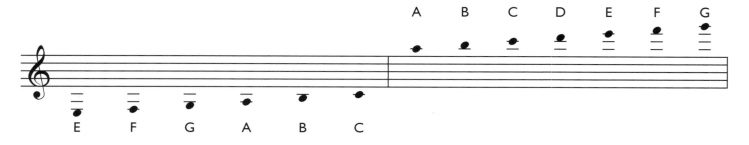

A B C D E F G

E F G A B C

Guitar music sounds one *octave* lower than it is written (an octave is the distance of 12 half steps between two pitches of the same name). We write the music an octave higher than it sounds strictly for reasons of convenience and easy reading.

FINGERINGS

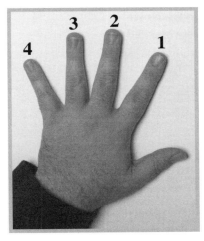

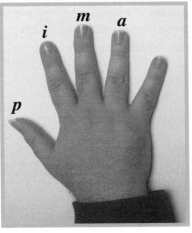

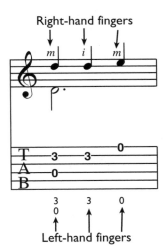

Numbers below the TAB represent the left-hand fingers used to fret the notes.

*The right-hand fingers, used to sound the strings, are represented by the letters **p i m** and **a**.*

READING CHORD AND FRETBOARD DIAGRAMS

A *chord* is three or more tones played simultaneously. A *Chord diagram* communicates the *shape* of a chord and how it is to be played. It is oriented vertically, so the strings are the vertical lines and the *frets* are the horizontal lines.

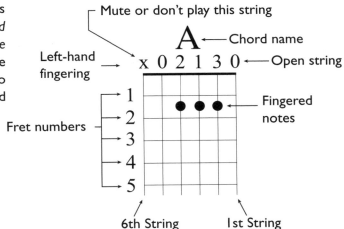

Fretboard diagrams are oriented horizontally. The horizontal lines are the strings and the vertical lines are the frets.

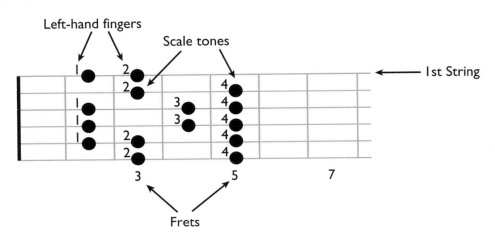

TIME

Musical time is measured in *beats*. The beats create the steady pulse of the music on which we build *rhythms*. Rhythm is the pattern of long and short sounds and silences and is represented by *note* and *rest values*. Value indicates duration.

NOTE VALUES

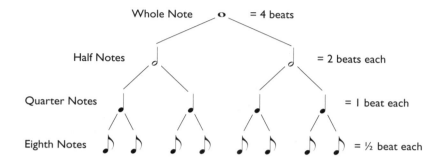

When alone, *eighth notes* appear with flags. When in groups, they are connected by *beams*.

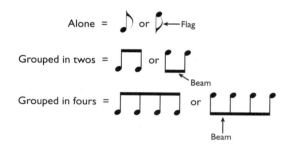

REST VALUES

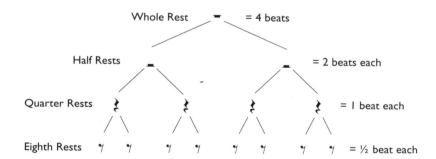

MEASURES AND BAR LINES

Beats are divided equally into *measures* (or *bars*) by vertical *bar lines*. The end of a section or example is marked by a *double bar line*.

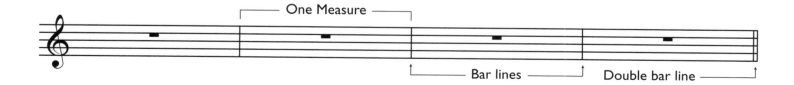

TIME SIGNATURES

A *time signature* appears at the beginning of a piece of music. The number on top indicates the number of beats per measure and the number on the bottom indicates the type of note getting one beat.

$$\frac{4}{4} =$$ Four beats per measure
Quarter note ♩ = one beat

$$\frac{3}{4} =$$ Three beats per measure
Quarter note ♩ = one beat

Sometimes a **C** is used in place of $\frac{4}{4}$.
This is called *common time.*

TIES AND DOTS

A *tie* is a curved line that joins two or more notes of the same pitch that last the duration of the combined note values. For example, when a *half note* (two beats) is tied to a *quarter note* (one beat) the combined notes are held for three beats (2 + 1 = 3).

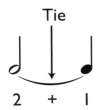

Tie

2   +   1

A *dot* after a note increases the note's value by half. For example, a *dotted half note* equals three beats because a half note equals two beats and half of its value is one beat (2 + 1 = 3). You can also think of the dotted half note as being equal to a half note tied to a quarter note. The same logic applies to any dotted note.

2 + 1 = 3   1 + ½ = 1½   4 + 2 = 6

*Algerian-born guitarist **Pierre Bensusan** has long been fascinated with his North African roots as well as the Celtic folk traditions of Western Europe. After making a name for himself as a folk musician in the late 1970s, Bensusan began to incorporate jazz and classical elements into his music, creating a virtuosic, highly original style on the acoustic guitar. He has arranged music as wide-ranging as classical orchestral music (Handel's* Water Music*) to Celtic classics such as* Shi Beg, Shi Mor.

HOW TO COUNT

This example is in $\frac{4}{4}$ time, so there are four beats in each measure. Try tapping your foot as you count aloud and clap your hands in the notated rhythm. Clap on the underlined counting numbers. The "&" symbols (ampersands) are said "and." Numbers in parentheses are rests.

This example is in $\frac{3}{4}$ time, so there are three beats in each measure. Tap your foot for three even beats per measure.

SIMPLE VS. COMPOUND METER

This example is in $\frac{6}{8}$ time. Most time signatures with the number 8 on the bottom are *compound meters,* meaning each beat is divisable into three even parts. Time signatures such as $\frac{4}{4}$ and $\frac{3}{4}$ are simple meters, meaning each beat is divisible into two parts. In example 3, count "1–&–ah, 2–&–ah," tapping your foot on "1" and "2."

POSTURE

Playing the guitar is far more athletic than you might expect. As with any physical activity, good posture is a key element to success. Taking the time to develop good habits at the beginning of your career will save you time later on; time you can apply to playing music instead of correcting bad habits.

Basic concepts which apply to all the positions shown below:

1. Both hands require easy access to the guitar and therefore must never be used to support the instrument.
2. The guitar should be held securely in a relaxed, comfortable position.
3. Avoid straining to reach the guitar.
4. Keep both wrists as straight as possible.
5. Avoid resting your left arm on your leg.

Folk.   *Classical.*   *Standing.*

LEFT HAND

The left hand should only touch the guitar neck with the thumb and the fingertips. The pad of the thumb should rest in the center of the back of the guitar neck. Gently curve the thumb outward; never bend the thumb in toward the 1st finger (see photo 1 below). The wrist may bend slightly inward or outward, but avoid any severe angle as this will result in undue stress. Keep the hand open and relaxed and do not rest the palm on the guitar neck.

When fretting the strings place the fingers as close to the frets as possible but never on top of the frets. You should be able to feel the frets beside the fingers (see photo 2 below).

Photo 1
Thumb behind the neck.

Photo 2
A good left-hand position.

Apply only as much pressure to the string as is required to get a clean sound. Over-pressing the string is a waste of valuable energy you will need to apply elsewhere.

RIGHT HAND

The right-hand fingers are responsible for *plucking* the strings. You can use bare fingers; or bare fingers and a *thumbpick;* or a thumbpick and *fingerpicks.* Thumb and fingerpicks slip on to your thumb and fingers and allow you to play fingerstyle while getting that crisp pick sound.

When plucking the string, all three joints should move in toward the palm. This should be done with the least possible hand or palm movement. Both the fingernail and the flesh are used simultaneously. Once the string is sounded, return the fingers to a ready position.

The thumb should be relaxed, extending outward from the hand. To pluck a string with the thumb, bring it downward toward the fingers with both joints. Do not bring the thumb into the palm under the fingers, as this will result in the fingers and thumb getting in each other's way.

Tone and volume are controlled by right-hand technique.

The right-hand position.

CHAPTER 2

Basic Arrangement

Below is a simple arrangement of the folk song "Billy The Kid." The *melody* (succession of single tones) and chords are included. Bare bones *arrangements* (versions) such as this one—called *lead sheets*—are commonly found in "fake books." Be careful, some books of this type abuse copyright laws and do not pay the songwriters. The arrangements in this book include TAB to make it easier for you to play the tune, but "fake books" rarely do. Also, notice that the song begins on the third beat, before the first beat of the first full measure. This is called a *pickup*.

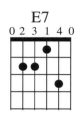
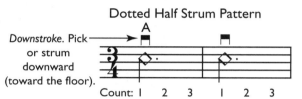
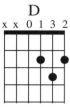

First play the melody to learn the tune. A sure sign that you have familiarized yourself with the melody is that you can sing it while strumming the chords. The chords you will need are shown on the right.

Remember the time signature is ¾. To the right is an example of the strum pattern you can use: *dotted half strums* (three beats each, one strum per measure). On the CD, the strums are on one channel and the melody is on the other. You can use your stereo's balance control to eliminate either part and play along.

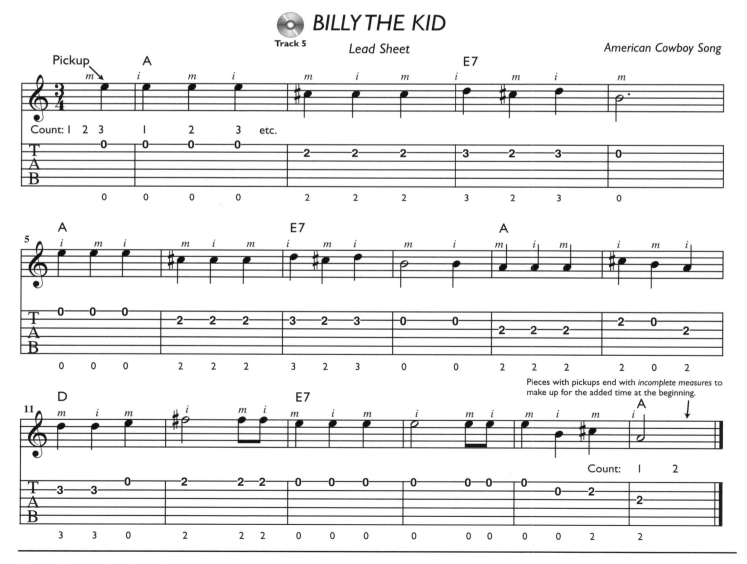

Once you are familiar with the melody and the chords, try this arrangement combining the melody with single bass notes. When playing this arrangement, get in the habit of fingering the chords you were strumming on page 16, even though you are only plucking single notes. As you progress as a player and arranger, this will enable you to spontaneously play additional notes from the chords.

This arrangement uses a *monotonic bass,* which is a simple but effective method of arranging a melody for fingerstyle guitar. The *roots* (pitches on which the chords are built) are played to identify the chords as they change. This is a forgiving arrangement in that all of the bass notes are played on open strings. Notice that in a *two-voice* (melody and bass) arrangement, bass notes have stems going down, and melody notes have stems going up. This makes the music clear and easy to read.

Track 6

BILLY THE KID

Monotonic Bass Arrangement

American Cowboy Song

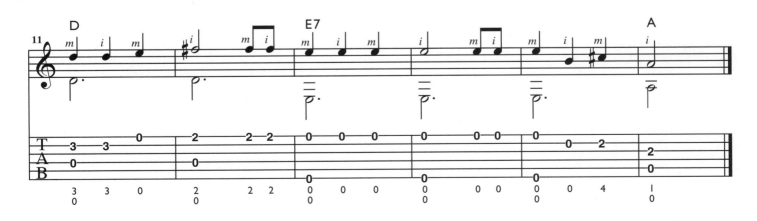

This arrangement of "Glory Glory (Since I've Laid My Burden Down)" uses a monotonic bass. The bass notes for the G and C chords must be fretted. Remember to hold down the chords as you move through the song.

Here are the chords you will need.

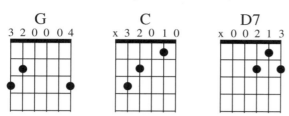

KEY SIGNATURE
This piece has a *key signature*, which is an accidental or group of accidentals at the beginning of every line of music showing which notes are sharp or flat throughout the piece. These are in effect in every octave unless cancelled with a natural sign.

GLORY GLORY
(SINCE I'VE LAID MY BURDEN DOWN)
Monotonic Bass

Track 7

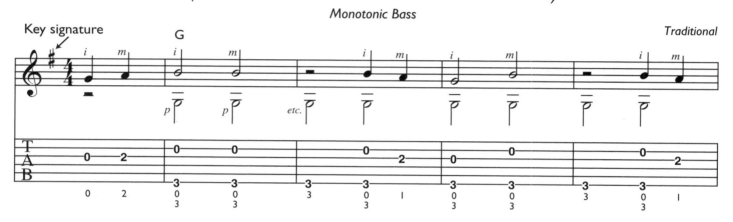

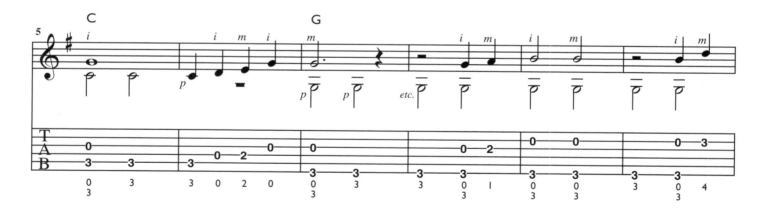

Block chords are a simple way to accompany a melody. In a block chord, all or most of the notes in the chord are strummed or plucked simultaneously.

BILLY THE KID

Track 8 *Block Chord Arrangement*

American Cowboy Song

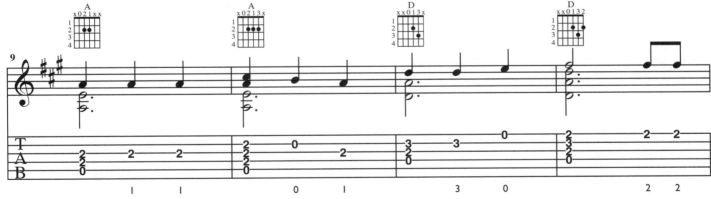

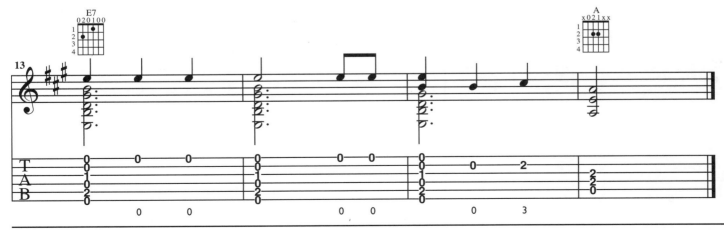

Here is another typical block chord arrangement.

GLORY GLORY
(SINCE I'VE LAID MY BURDEN DOWN)

Track 9

Traditional

Block Chord Arrangement

CHAPTER 3

The Major Scale and Chord Theory

A *scale* is group of pitches arranged in a specific order of whole steps (W) and half steps (H), often referred to as a *formula*. Different formulas give us different scales. The *major scale* is typically learned first as it is the standard by which many other musical concepts are defined. The formula used to build it is: **W–W–H–W–W–W–H**.

Using this formula, a major scale can be built from any pitch. Below is a *C Major scale*. Notice that the TAB shows the scale on the 5th string only; it is easiest to see the order of whole steps and half steps on one string.

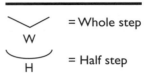

= Whole step

= Half step

C Major Scale

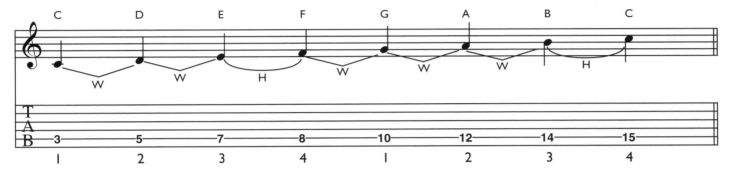

The first pitch in the scale is called the *tonic*. Each consecutive pitch is referred to as a *scale degree*; D is the 2nd degree (2), E is the 3rd degree (3), etc.

C is the only major scale with no sharps or flats. All other major scales use either sharps or flats (never both!) to maintain the formula. Here is a chart showing the names of the pitches in all of the major scales.

Tonic	W	2	W	3	H	4	W	5	W	6	W	7	H	Tonic [1]
C		D		E		F		G		A		B		C
G		A		B		C		D		E		F♯		G
D		E		F♯		G		A		B		C♯		D
A		B		C♯		D		E		F♯		G♯		A
E		F♯		G♯		A		B		C♯		D♯		E
B		C♯		D♯		E		F♯		G♯		A♯		B
F♯		G♯		A♯		B		C♯		D♯		E♯ [2]		F♯
C♯		D♯		E♯ [2]		F♯		G♯		A♯		B♯ [3]		C♯
F		G		A		B♭		C		D		E		F
B♭		C		D		E♭		F		G		A		B♭
E♭		F		G		A♭		B♭		C		D		E♭
A♭		B♭		C		D♭		E♭		F		G		A♭
D♭		E♭		F		G♭		A♭		B♭		C		D♭
G♭		A♭		B♭		C♭ [4]		D♭		E♭		F		G♭
C♭ [4]		D♭		E♭		F♭ [5]		G♭		A♭		B♭		C♭ [4]

[1] An octave (12 half steps) above the initial tonic.

[2] E♯ is the enharmonic equivalent of F♮.

[3] B♯ is the enharmonic equivalent of C♮.

[4] C♭ is the enharmonic equivalent of B♮.

[5] F♭ is the enharmonic equivalent of E♮.

INTERVALS

As mentioned on page 21, the major scale is used as a standard by which other musical concepts are understood. To use the scale this way, it is important to understand *intervals*. An interval is the distance between two pitches. You already know two intervals: the whole step and the half step.

Every pitch in a major scale can be understood in terms of its interval from the tonic. The second degree, for example, is an interval of a 2nd (2) above the tonic. The third degree is an interval of a 3rd (3) above the tonic, and so on. The same note sounded more than once is a *unison*.

P = Perfect
M = Major

Every interval has a *quality*. It is either *major*, *minor*, *perfect*, *diminished* or *augmented*. All of the pitches in a major scale, when measured from the tonic, create perfect or major intervals.

A major interval can be changed to a minor interval using an accidental. For example, C–E is a major 3rd, so C–E♭ is a minor 3rd. Other intervals can be changed this way too.

CHORD THEORY: MAJOR AND MINOR TRIADS

Remember, a chord is the combination of three (or more) different notes. The most basic chords are three-note chords called *triads*. *Major* and *minor triads* are the most commonly used chords. Triads are built by stacking pitches in 3rds.

Let's build a C Major triad. C is the *root* (1) of the chord; E is a 3rd above C, so it is called the *3rd* (3) of the chord; G is a 3rd above E and a 5th above C, so it is called the 5th (5) of the chord.

m = Minor

You can use the 1, 3 and 5 of any major scale to build a major triad. Lower the 3rd (♭3) of any major triad, or you can think in terms of lowering the 3rd of the scale, and you have a minor triad. Notice that it is a minor 3rd from the 1 to the ♭3 and a major 3rd from the ♭3 to the 5.

Other common chord formulas are shown below. Notice the new intervals: d5 (smaller than perfect) and A5 (larger than perfect). Also notice that the "7" chord is not a triad; it has four notes.

A = Augmented
d = Diminished

C Diminished
1 - ♭3 - ♭5
C - E♭ - G♭

C Augumented
1 - 3 - #5
C - E - G#

C7
1 - 3 - 5 - ♭7
C - E - G - B♭

Diatonic means belonging to the scale. Each note in a scale has a corresponding triad. These are the diatonic triads of the scale.

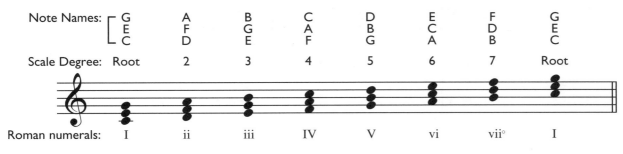

I or i	1
II or ii	2
III or iii	3
IV or iv	4
V or v	5
VI or vi	6
VII or vii	7

Roman numerals are used to represent each chord. Uppercase is used for major chords (I, IV, V—also known as the *primary chords*) and lowercase is used for minor and diminished chords (ii, iii, vi, vii). This sign ∘ is used to show that a chord is diminished (vii°).

The series of diatonic chords is the same for all major scales.

I	ii	iii	IV	V	vi	vii°	I
major	minor	minor	major	major	minor	diminished	major

Different major scales and the chords that come from them are called *keys*. For example, if the melody and chords of a song come from the D Major scale, it is "in the key of D."

Below is a chart showing the names of the pitches in all the major scales. At the top of each column is the Roman numeral for each chord. Using this chart, you can find the name of any diatonic triad in any major scale or key. For example, the ii chord in the key of E Major is an F♯ Minor chord.

I	ii	iii	IV	V	vi	vii°
C	D	E	F	G	A	B
G	A	B	C	D	E	F♯
D	E	F♯	G	A	B	C♯
A	B	C♯	D	E	F♯	G♯
E	F♯	G♯	A	B	C♯	D♯
B	C♯	D♯	E	F♯	G♯	A♯
F♯	G♯	A♯	B	C♯	D♯	E♯
C♯	D♯	E♯	F♯	G♯	A♯	B♯
F	G	A	B♭	C	D	E
B♭	C	D	E♭	F	G	A
E♭	F	G	A♭	B♭	C	D
A♭	B♭	C	D♭	E♭	F	G
D♭	E♭	F	G♭	A♭	B♭	C
G♭	A♭	B♭	C♭	D♭	E♭	F
C♭	D♭	E♭	F♭	G♭	A♭	B♭

CHAPTER 4

Travis Picking & Alternating Bass

The concept of alternating the bass notes between the root and the 5th of the chord is commonly called *Travis picking* after Merle Travis, who used this "boom-chick" technique extensively in his guitar style. In $\frac{4}{4}$ time, beats 1 and 3 ("boom") are typically the root, and beats 2 and 4 ("chick") are the 5th. Playing these notes with your thumb and putting a little snap on the "chick" can really propel a tune.

GETTING THAT TRAVIS SOUND

Mastering Travis picking is essential to developing fingerstyle guitar technique. It is the foundation on which many fingerstyle arrangements are built. The objective here is to create the illusion of two or more guitars/instruments.

ACCOMPANIMENT: BASS AND DRUMS

Try using a thumb pick and *palm muting* the bass strings with the heel of your right hand. Many blues players choose to do this—and on the CD, this is what you will hear—but it is optional for this book. Palm muting is done by placing the heel of your hand where the strings join the bridge, to muffle the bass strings (see photo 1 below).

Think of yourself as being a drum set. The palm mute on beats 1 and 3 gives you the sound of a kick drum ("boom") (see photo 2 below).

Then, lean into beats 2 and 4 for the "chick" and get that snare drum sound. Varying the amount you mute the bass strings will adjust the tone of your virtual drum kit (see photo 3 below).

Photo 1
Palm muting.

Photo 2
"Boom" = Kick. Palm muted thumb stroke on 6th string.

Photo 3
"Chick" = Snare. Palm muted thumb stroke on 4th string.

Below is an example applying an alternating bass over some familiar chords. Notice how the roots are played on the "boom" beats (1 and 3) and the 5ths are on the "chick" beats (2 and 4).

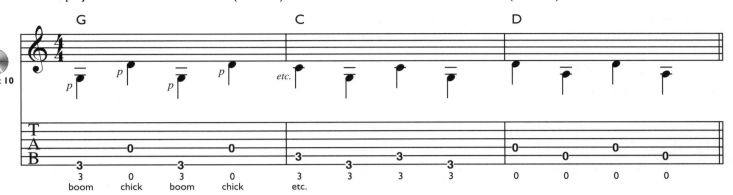

MELODY

The melody is generally played on the top three strings. Let the strings ring out so you can hear the melody over the accompaniment.

You are trying to simulate the sound of a complete band. With practice, you will learn to adjust the volume levels of the parts of your arrangement. Giving the accompaniment and the melody different tonal characteristics will help create the illusion of more than one guitar/instrument.

Try alternating the bass notes of a G Major chord over a G Major scale, as in example 5.

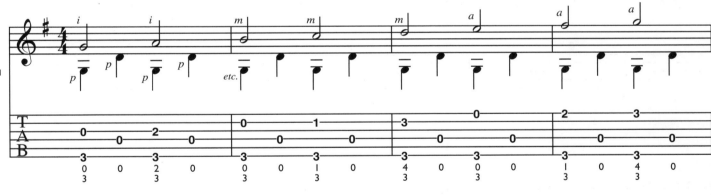

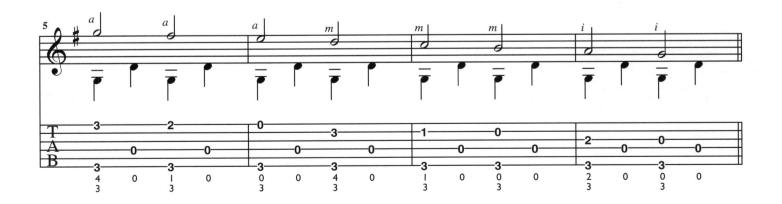

Here is an exercise for practicing palm muting while playing the *chromatic scale*. "Chromatic" is the term used to refer to movement by half step. The chromatic scale has all 12 pitches in an octave.

Using the 2nd and 3rd fingers of your left hand to hold the bass notes for a G chord, use your 1st and 4th fingers to play the chromatic scale. This is a real workout for the left hand.

Observe the left-hand fingerings under the TAB; these will guide your use of the 1st and 4th finger in playing the scale.

Try this arrangement of "Glory Glory" with an alternating bass. Remember to hold the chords down as you move through the song and pay attention to the left-hand fingerings underneath the TAB. Most of the melody notes are found within the chords but you must use the 1st finger of your left hand to play the A-note while holding the G Major chord.

GLORY GLORY
(SINCE I'VE LAID MY BURDEN DOWN)

Track 13

Alternating Bass Arrangement

Traditional

Try this arrangement of "Billy the Kid." This song is in $\frac{3}{4}$ time, so the bass alternates with the root on beat 1 and the 5th on beats 2 and 3. The sound of this bass is "boom–chick–chick."

BILLY THE KID

Track 14 *Alternating Bass Arrangement*

American Cowboy Song

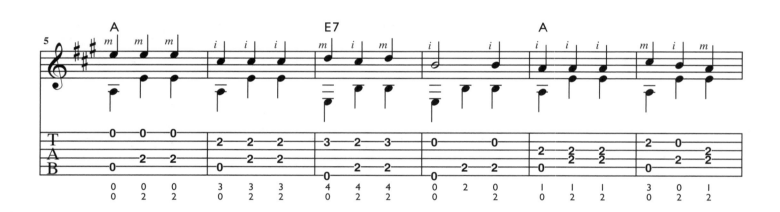

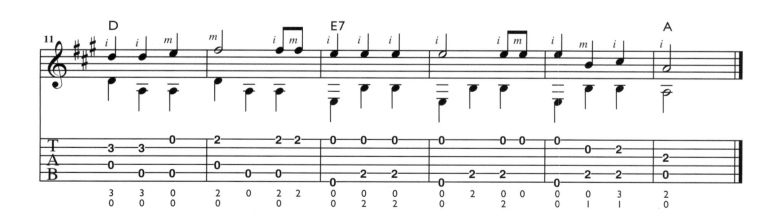

CHAPTER 5

Ear Candy

SYNCOPATION

Syncopation is the shifting of the emphasis from the strong parts of beats (the *onbeats*) to the weak parts (the *offbeats*). It creates rhythms which are essential to playing contemporary styles of music including rock, blues and jazz. In fingerstyle guitar, syncopated melodies are often played against an unsyncopated alternating bass.

In the following examples 7 and 8, we will convert a straight melody to a syncopated one.

In this example, all of the melody notes (stems up) are played on the beat.

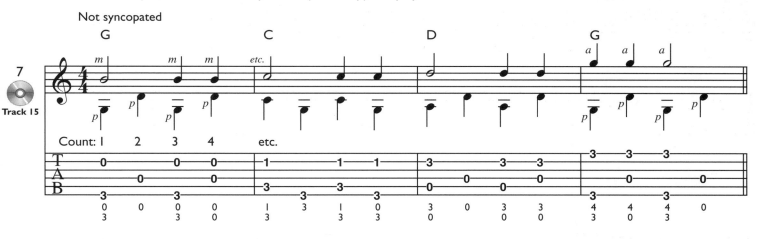

In this example, the melody notes have been syncopated by shifting them to offbeats.

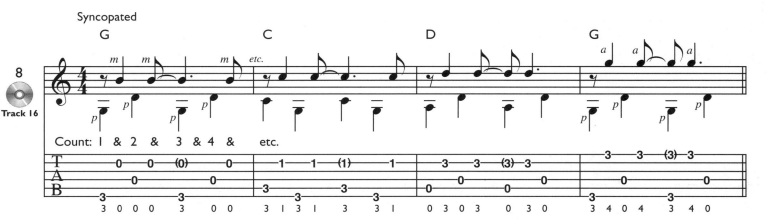

Notice that some of the notes have been played after the beat and some have been shifted before the beat.

GLORY GLORY
(SINCE I'VE LAID MY BURDEN DOWN)

Syncopated Melody

Traditional

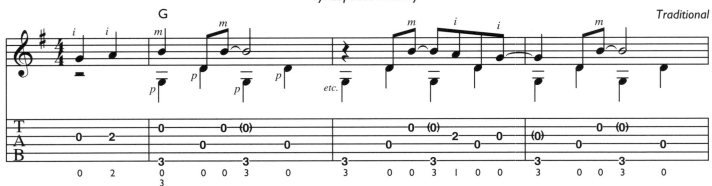

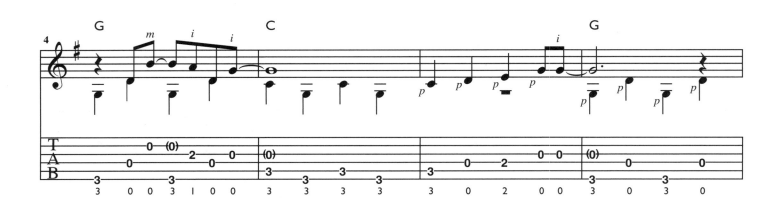

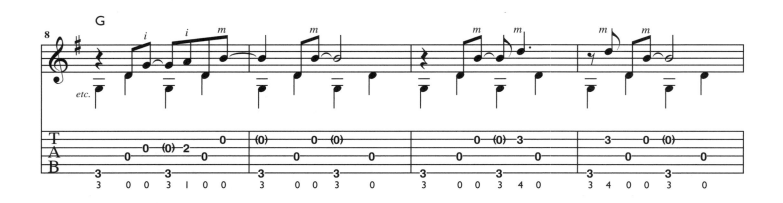

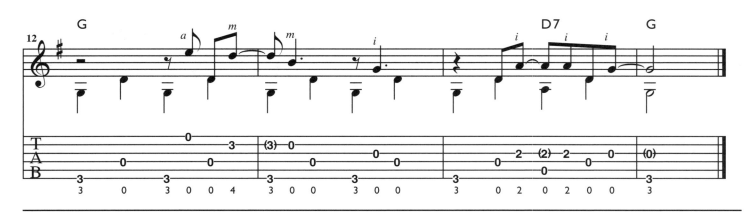

PICKING PATTERNS

Here are two right-hand picking patterns commonly used to develop arrangements. Practice these patterns slowly so that the left hand can play them effortlessly.

The A Minor chord, shown at the right, is used in these examples.

PICKING PATTERN NO. 1: *pm–p–i–p–m–p*

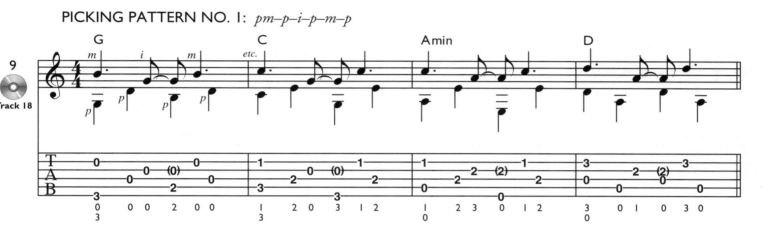

PICKING PATTERN NO. 2: *p–m–p–i–p–m–p–i*

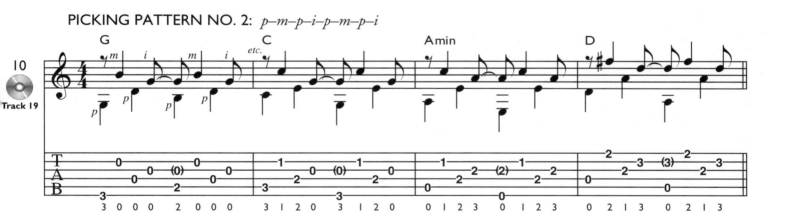

By adjusting the right-hand picking pattern and the left-hand chord shapes, these patterns can be used as the accompaniment in a fingerstyle arrangement. The right hand may have to alter the string or time of the pattern to accommodate the melody and the left hand may have to alter the chord shape to accommodate melody notes outside of the chord.

Below is an arrangement of the traditional tune, "Corrinna, Corrinna," using a pattern based on Picking Pattern No.1 (page 31). For this you will need to learn the F chord. This is a *barre chord,* which means that one of your fingers (in this case, your 1st finger) will fret more than one string at the same time. Observe the chord chart to the right: Lay your 1st finger across all the strings at the 1st fret and then place your 3rd, 4th and 2nd fingers. In the song below, the 5th string is not used in the F chord, so you can use the alternate fingering in the diagram to the far right. If you have never played barre chords before, it may take some practice, so be patient.

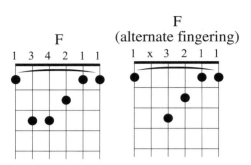

CORRINNA, CORRINNA

Track 20

Traditional

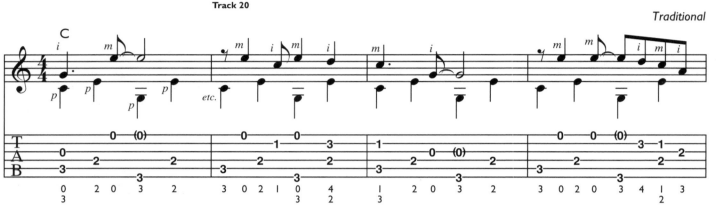

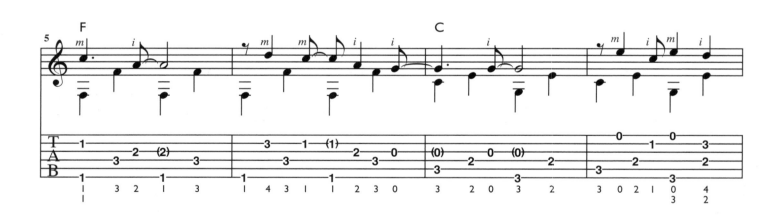

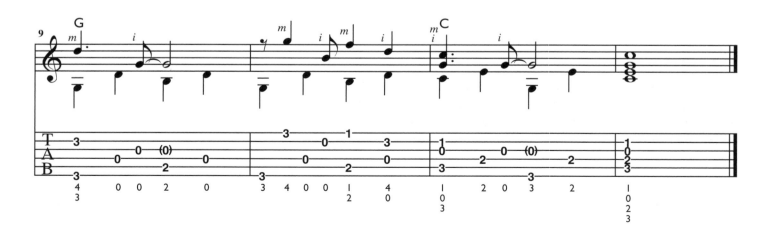

PICKING PATTERN NO. 3: *p–i–m–a–m–i*

Here is a common picking pattern in ¾ time. Notice it has a descending bass line. Keep your 1st finger on the C-note on the 1st fret of the 2nd string throughout. Also notice the use of *slash chords*. A slash chord indicates that a note other than the root is in the bass, or even a note not belonging to the chord. The chord symbol is to the left of the slash, and the bass note is to the right.

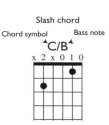
Slash chord

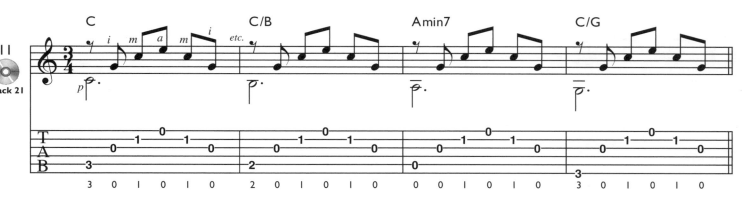

TRIPLETS

A *triplet* is three notes in the time of two. The most commonly used triplet is the *eighth-note triplet,* which is three eighth notes in the time of two, or three eighth notes per beat. Say "tri-pa-let" while tapping your foot. Every time your foot hits the floor, start the first syllable. That's the triplet feel. Another way to count eighth-note triplets is "1–&–ah, 2–&–ah," and so on.

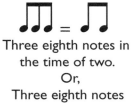

Three eighth notes in
the time of two.
Or,
Three eighth notes
per beat.

PICKING PATTERN NO. 4: *p–i–m–pa–m–i*

Here is a picking pattern with triplets. This example is based on the pattern in example 11, above. Here, the bass plays quarter notes while triplets are played above.

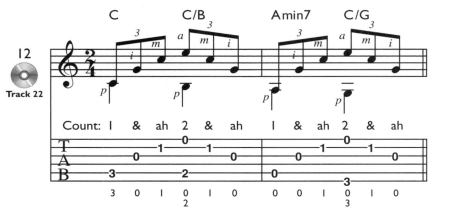

The tune below has lots of triplets over an alternating bass. This should keep your right hand busy. Notice that it uses lots of new chords; diagrams are provided for each. Practice each new chord separately before working on the song.

Z RHYMES WITH NED

Track 23

Walking bass lines are created by moving the bass through a scale. These bass notes are often chosen to connect the chords in a *progression* (series of chords). Sometimes the bass notes are used to imply alternate chords. We will discuss this later when looking at *reharmonizing* a chord progression with *chord substitutions* (page 66).

Here is a basic walking bass line in the key of C (all of the notes are from the C Major scale).

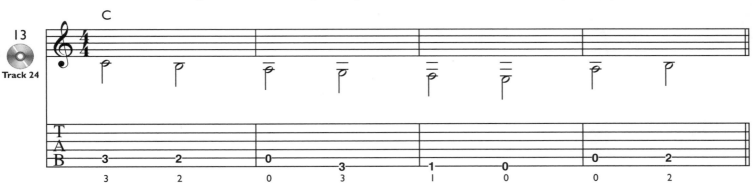

Here is the same walking bass line with a common picking pattern: *p–m–p–i–p–m–p–i*.

Here is a repeated walking bass arrangement of "Frere Jacques." Observe the suggested left-hand fingerings. These should help you navigate both the melody and the bass parts.

FRÈRE JACQUES

Track 26 *Walking Bass Arrangement*

French Traditional

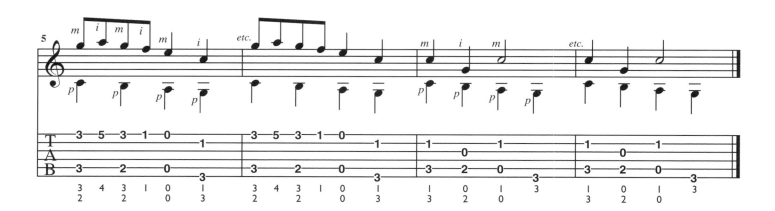

Martin Simpson (b. 1953) is one of the most gifted fingerstyle guitarist/arrangers on the scene today. His varied repertoire includes arrangements of traditional Celtic and blues tunes, as well his original compositions.

HARMONIZING IN 3RDS

A great arranging tool for fingerstyle guitar is to *harmonize* the melody. To harmonize is to add intervals (page 22) to the melody. Many consider 3rds to be the most agreeable of intervals for harmonizing a melody. This will require the use of higher notes written above the staff on ledger lines (see page 8).

Below are the diatonic (see page 23) 3rds of a C Major scale.

Notice we used two types of 3rds to harmonize the major scale, the major 3rd (M3) and the minor 3rd (m3). In a major 3rd, the notes are two whole steps apart. In a minor 3rd, the notes are one-and-a-half steps apart. Here are fingering shapes for both types of 3rds, one set for playing on the 1st and 2nd strings (String Set 1–2), another for the 2nd and 3rd strings (String Set 2–3). Alternate fingerings are in parentheses.

String Set 1–2

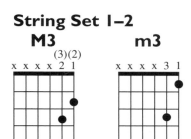

String Set 2–3

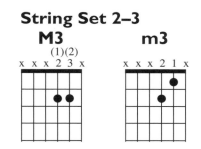

Notice these 3rds mirror the pattern of a major scale harmonized with triads (see page 23).

Harmonized 3rds	M3	m3	m3	M3	M3	m3	m3
Diatonic Triads	Major I	Minor ii	Minor iii	Major IV	Major V	Minor vi	Diminished vii°

In the case of the seventh chord (vii°), remember that a diminished triad has a minor 3rd.

Here is the melody to "Corrina, Corrina" harmonized in 3rds.

CORRINNA, CORRINNA

Track 27

Melody Harmonized in 3rds

Traditional

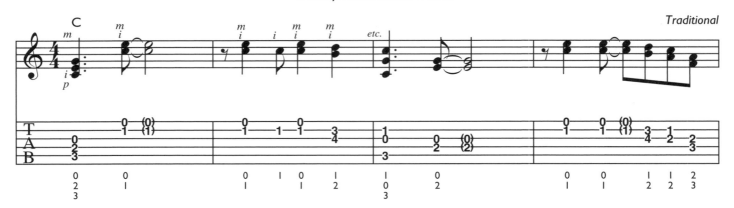

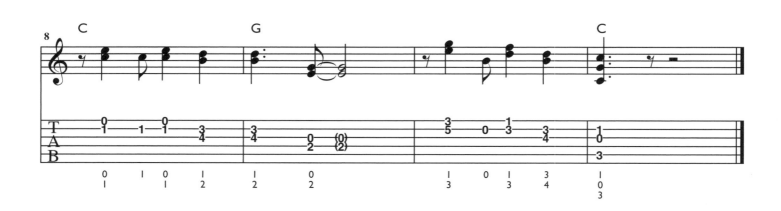

HARMONIZING IN 6THS

Another very agreeable interval to use when harmonizing a melody is the 6th.

Here is the C Major scale harmonized in 6ths.

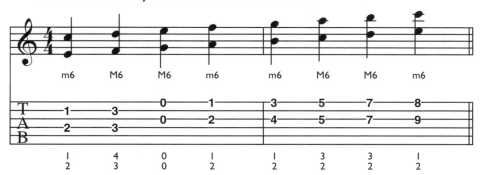

6ths are *inverted* 3rds. To invert an interval, the note on the bottom is moved to the top, or vice versa. For example, when the E is above the C, the notes form a major 3rd (a distance of four half steps); when the E is below the C, the notes form a minor 6th (a distance of eight half steps).

Below are eight diagrams for playing 6ths. Notice that the shapes of the respective fingerings are the same on each pair of string sets. When playing "Corrinna, Corrinna" on page 40, try using the fingerings below. Use the 2nd finger of your left hand to play the low note and shift between minor and major 6ths using your 1st and 3rd fingers, respectively.

The shapes in the top row are for 6ths played on the 4th and 2nd strings and the 3rd and 1st strings (String Sets 4–2 and 3–1). The shapes in the bottom row are for 6ths played on the 6th and 4th strings and the 5th and 3rd strings (String Sets 6–4 and 5–3).

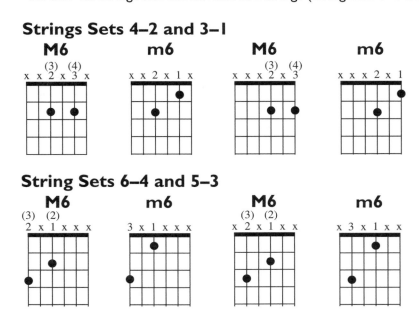

Here is the melody of "Corrinna, Corrinna" harmonized in 6ths.

CORRINNA, CORRINNA
Melody Harmonized in 6ths

Traditional

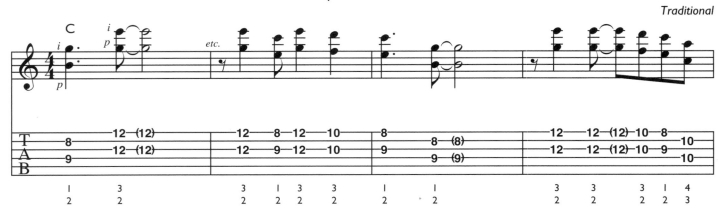

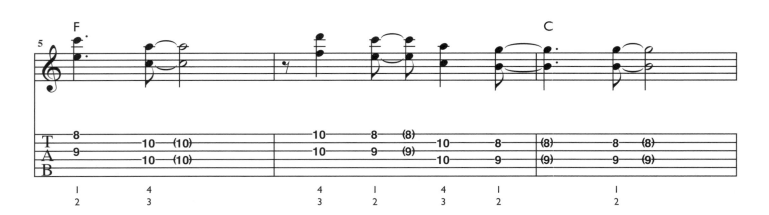

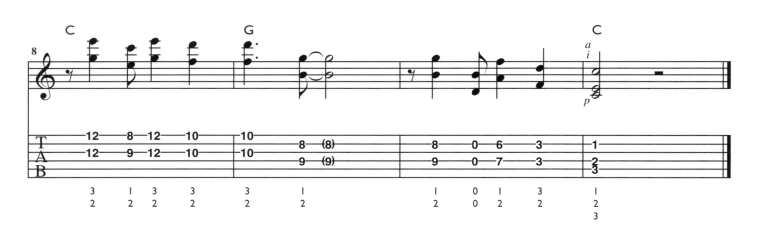

MUSICAL EXPRESSION

Great musicians *express* themselves when they play. This requires more than just playing all the right notes and chords. Here are some things to consider when trying to make a piece of music "your own."

DYNAMICS

Dynamics refers to the softness or loudness of the music that is being played. Dynamics should vary throughout an arrangement; when expressing yourself in conversation, you rarely speak at one constant level. Try playing your arrangements as softly as you can, then as loudly as you can. Then play them with dynamic variations that sound good to you. With practice your dynamic range will increase.

TIMBRE

Timbre (TAM-br) refers to *tone color,* or the quality of the sound. Often, guitarists get caught up in the gear aspect of timbre, placing the responsibility of tone-control on equipment alone. A great deal of tonal control, however, lies in how we *play* our guitar. Plucking the string near the bridge *(sul ponticello)* gives us a twangy, bright sound; the tone gets richer the closer we get to the neck *(sul tasto)*. For a more percussive sound, try muting the bass strings by resting the palm of your right hand where the bridge meets the bass strings (see page 24).

TEMPO

This is the speed at which a song is played. *Tempo* has considerable effect on the mood of a performance. Experiment with various tempos for each arrangement; some songs even benefit from tempo-variation within a performance.

Listen intently to great players you admire and take note of how they use these forms of musical expression to "bend" your ear. Attend live performances and observe how performers can control the mood in the room through the use of these devices.

When working on a song, first make sure all technical aspects are in place (the right notes and chords at the right time), then work on these forms of musical expression. This is the icing on the cake and can make all the difference to your audience (and yourself).

CHAPTER 6

Left-Hand Techniques

Many left-hand techniques were developed to create *legato* (smooth, connected) sounds on our plucked-string instruments; notations for such techniques involve a *slur* ⌢. Slurs look similar to ties (page 11), but the notes tied together are different pitches.

PULL-OFFS

The *pull-off* is a descending legato accomplished by plucking the first note then pulling the left-hand finger off the string to activate the lower note without plucking. Rather than simply lifting your finger directly off the string, pull across the string with a downward (toward the floor) motion. This will help to sound the string. It will take some practice to do this without bumping the adjacent string.

P = Pull-off

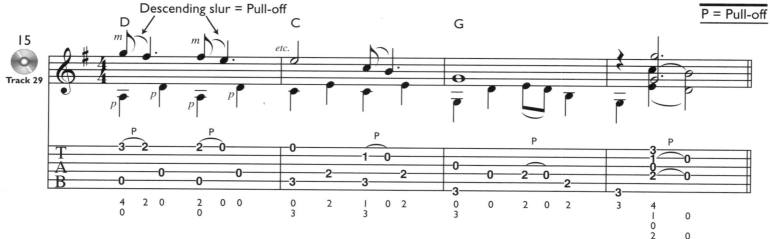

HAMMER-ONS

The *hammer-on* is the reverse of the pull-off. Pluck the first note with your right hand, then use your left-hand finger to "hammer-on" to the second note on the same string. This technique is very tricky at first; often the second note does not have much volume. Make sure you hammer-on with the tip of your finger as close to the fret as possible. To train your left-hand fingers, try sounding only the second note with just your left hand.

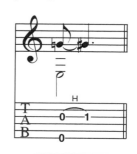

H = Hammer-on

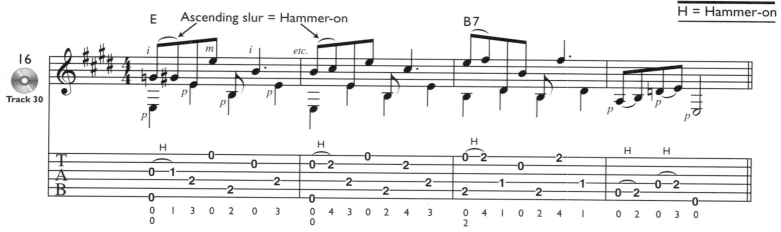

For both of these techniques, it is important that your fingers move in a quick and assertive fashion or you will mute the strings rather than slur the notes. Another common problem when first learning slurs is *rushing* (playing certain notes too fast). Remember to give the notes their proper value. If you are having trouble with rhythm in your slurs, try this:

Step 1: Play the music while counting aloud *without* the slurs until you have mastered the rhythm.
Step 2: Play the music *with* the slurs (still counting aloud).

After you have taken this two-step approach with a few songs, you will have a better feel for slurs and be able to omit the first step.

Below is an arrangement of "A-Tisket, A-Tasket" using hammer-ons and pull-offs. Observe the left-hand fingerings below the TAB. Your 4th finger is going to get a workout here. Also take note of instances where you are pulling-off or hammering-on to a note that coincides with a bass note played by your right-hand thumb, as in measure 2. This will take practice, but be sure that all notes are held for their full value and that the dynamic level is maintained on these notes.

A-TISKET, A-TASKET

Track 31

Traditional

SWINGING THE EIGHTHS

In some styles of music, most notably jazz and blues, musicians often (almost always!) "swing the eighths." Swing feel is easiest to explain in relation to triplets. Two swung eighth notes will sound similar to a triplet with the first two notes tied: long–short, long–short.

Swing 8ths

Swing eighth notes, however, look no different than ordinary eighth notes; it's just something musicians do to the rhythm. And since the rhythm described above is only an approximation of swung eighth notes, they are impossible to notate. The only way to really learn how to swing is to listen to musicians swingin'. Listen to any good jazz musician play and you'll get the idea.

In this book, this swing feel will be indicated at the beginning of a song with: *Swing 8ths.*

Using a *slide* (*glissando*) to create legato from one note to the next is a great way to personalize a phrase. Listen to recordings in any style of music on just about every instrument, and you will hear musicians using slides to express themselves with gliding, almost vocal sounds.

A slide is accomplished by shifting the position of your hand along the fretboard and gliding along the string. Do not lift your finger when sliding or you will mute the string and your sliding note stop. It will take some practice to apply just the required amount of pressure on the string to make the note ring clearly as you slide. Make sure to use a finger that puts you in a good position to continue playing *after* the slide.

Slides are indicated with a slur and a line connecting the notes; upward lines for slides ascending the string and downward slides for slides descending the string.

SL = Slide

PORTAMENTO SLIDES

A *portamento* slide involves two distinct notes with each note clearly heard and given its own rhythmic value. The note you are sliding to should be arrived at on time, which means you may have to borrow some time from the first note. Here is a blues lick with a monotonic bass (page 17) and slides.

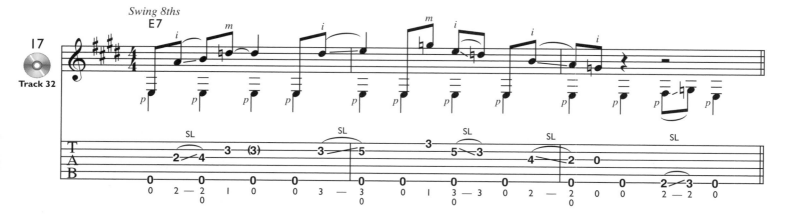

GRACE-NOTE SLIDES

A *grace note* is a small note ♪ played quickly before the main, target note. It is used as an *embellishment*. The grace note should not be heard distinctly and its rhythmic value should be borrowed from the target note. Example 18 is a similar blues lick to example 17, but this time it has grace-note slides.

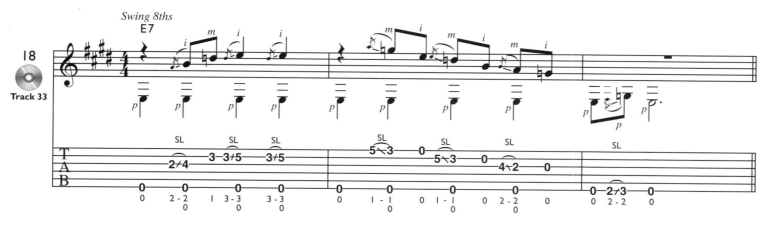

Here is a blues tune with a monotonic bass. By the time you get this one under your fingers, you'll be a slur master!

A BOOT MY SIZE

Track 34

CHAPTER 7

Harmonics

Harmonics are distinctive bell-like tones we can create to add interest to our arrangements.

LEFT-HAND HARMONIC TECHNIQUE

To create a harmonic:

- Place the 1st finger of your left hand directly above the 12th fret of the 1st string.

- Touch the string very lightly—just enough to feel the tension of the string. Do not press the string down onto the fretboard.

- Pluck the string with your right hand and immediately lift your left-hand finger off the string.

Correct.

Incorrect.

It may take some practice to get clean-sounding harmonics. Here are some things to consider:

- Although you normally fret a note just *behind* the fret, for harmonics your finger must be directly *above* the fret wire.

- You may be plucking in a bit of a "dead spot"; try plucking somewhere else. Don't move far away, maybe a distance equal to the width of your fingertip.

- Adjust (probably lessen) the amount of pressure you are putting on the string with your left-hand finger.

- Lifting your left-hand finger too fast will cause the string to ring open.

- Lifting your left-hand finger too slow will mute the string.

- Fingernails and picks work much better than flesh for striking the strings.

Once you are able to consistently play a clear harmonic at the 12th fret, it is time to learn where the other harmonics are located. These locations are called *nodes*. The example below shows the most commonly used nodes: the 12th, 7th, 5th and 9th frets. Harmonics are designated by diamond-shaped noteheads in the standard music notation and, in this book, diamonds above the TAB.

◆ ◇ = Harmonics

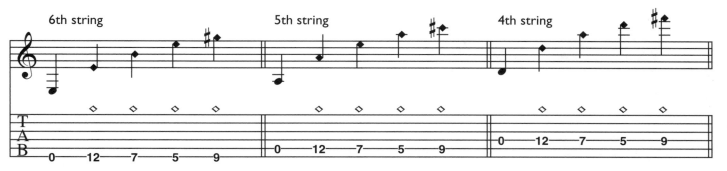

8*va* = *Ottava alta.* Sounds an octave higher than written.

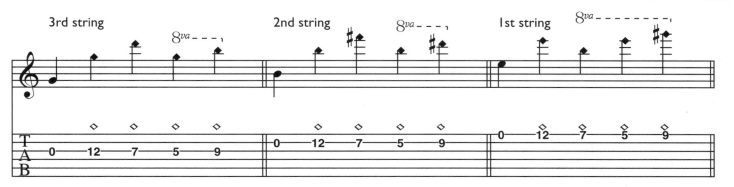

When a regular note—such as an open string—is played, it gives us the *fundamental tone*. The harmonics on that string will give us pitches from the *overtone series**. Happily, most of these relate to the major triad which would be built from the fundamental. For example: the open 1st string is E and the harmonics above it are all found in the E Major triad (E–G♯–B): the 12th fret harmonic = E; 7th fret = B; 5th fret = E; 9th fret = G♯. Below is a chart showing the names and locations of the harmonics for each open string.

	Open-String Harmonics				
	Fundamental	**Root**	**5th**	**Root**	**Major 3rd**
			Harmonic at		
String	**Open Note**	**12th Fret**	**7th Fret**	**5th Fret**	**9th Fret**
1	E	E	B	E	G♯
2	B	B	F♯	B	D♯
3	G	G	D	G	B
4	D	D	A	D	F♯
5	A	A	E	A	C♯
6	E	E	B	E	G♯

* Every musical pitch contains an array of pitches which combine to create the pitch we hear and the timbre or *color* of the sound. This is very much like light: When we view any light through a prism, we discover that it can be broken into a rainbow of colors. In a sense, harmonics are a musical prism and *overtones* (harmonics) are the colors that combine to make the pitch we hear.

Here is an arrangement of the old folk song, "Michael, Row the Boat Ashore," played almost exclusively with harmonics. Notice the C-note in the fifth bar will have to be fretted because there is no open-string C harmonic in standard tuning.

MICHAEL, ROW THE BOAT ASHORE

Harmonics

Track 35

Traditional

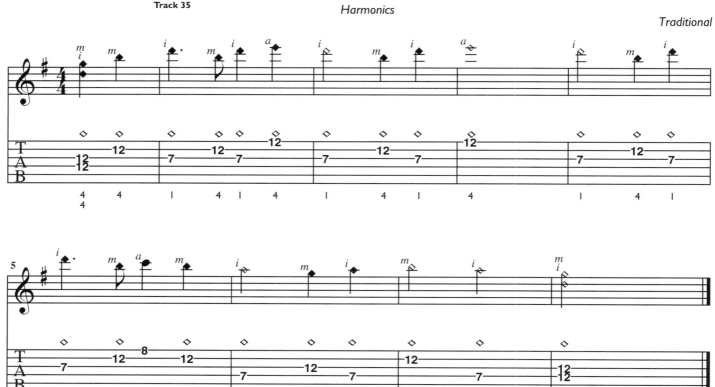

Michael Hedges was arguably the most innovative acoustic guitarist of the 20th century. His brilliant solo guitar compositions included the use of colorful, uniquely applied techniques such as left- and right-hand tapping, harmonics and various percussive effects.

RIGHT-HAND HARMONIC TECHNIQUES

Right-hand harmonic technique allows you to find the node and pluck the string using only your right hand. Here is how it is done:

- Place *i* (right-hand index finger) on the node above the 12th fret on the 1st string.
- Use *p* (right-hand thumb) or *a* (right-hand ring finger) to pluck the 1st string.
- Lift *i* away from the node as quickly as possible.

*Using **p** (with thumbpick) to pluck the string.*

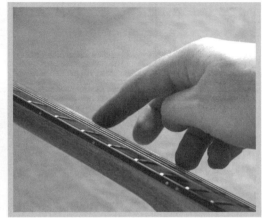

*Using **a** to pluck the string.*

Go back and try playing all those harmonics you learned on the 12th, 7th, 5th and 9th frets using this technique.

ARTIFICIAL HARMONICS

Artificial harmonics are played by combining fretted notes and the right-hand harmonic technique. To do this, we use the *i* finger to touch a node 12, 7, 5 or 9 frets above the fretted note. The string is then struck with *p* or *a* as described above.

Here is an example of how it is done:

- With the 1st finger of your left hand, hold the F on the 1st fret of 1st string. The octave node has now moved up one fret from the 12th to the 13th fret.
- Use the right-hand harmonic technique to play the node at the 13th fret.

As with an open-string harmonic at the 12th fret, the pitch you hear will sound one octave above the note you fret.

To help you locate the nodes used in this technique, think of the 12th fret as a "virtual" nut and then visualize the nodes above it. The node will be located 12 frets above the note you are fretting with your left hand. For example, if you hold down the string at the 3rd fret, the node will move to the 15th fret (12+3=15). If you hold down the string at the 5th fret, the node will move to the 17th fret (12+5=17).

Here is the melody to "Greensleeves" with artificial harmonics. This should give you plenty of practice in visualizing melodies above the virtual nut.

GREENSLEEVES

Artificial Harmonics

Traditional English Melody

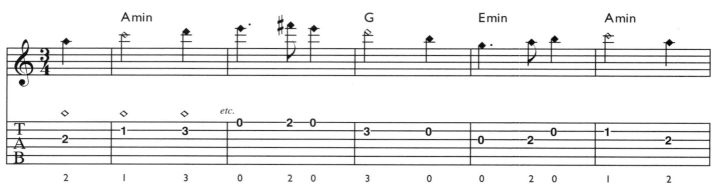

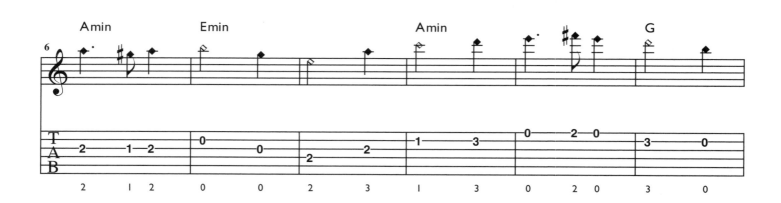

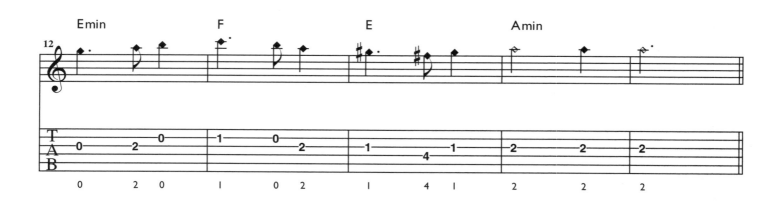

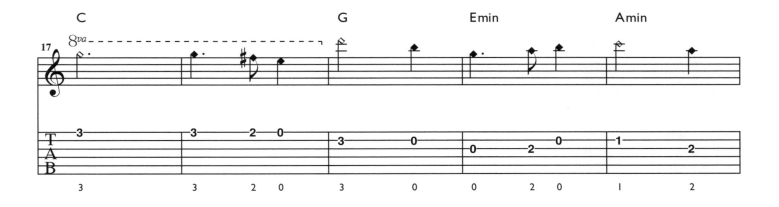

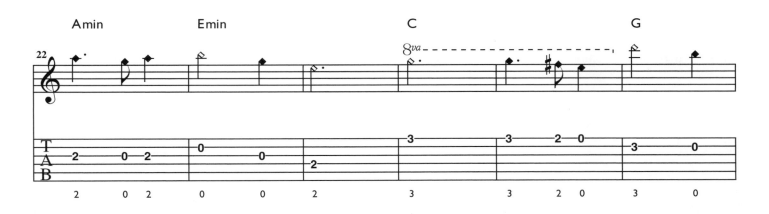

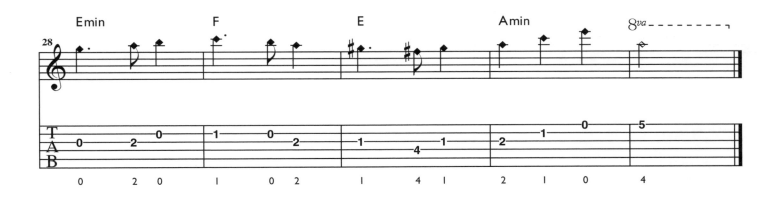

"Kissing Bells" has a common chord progression. Bars 5 to 7 use some new chord *voicings* (how notes are arranged in chords). Here they are:

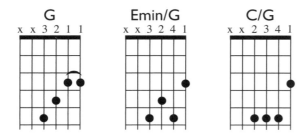

When playing "Kissing Bells," hold down the chords as you visualize them above the virtual nut. To find the nodes, remember to add 12 frets to the fret you are holding with your left hand. Then trace the chords with your right hand to sound the harmonics.

KISSING BELLS

Track 37 *Artificial Harmonics*

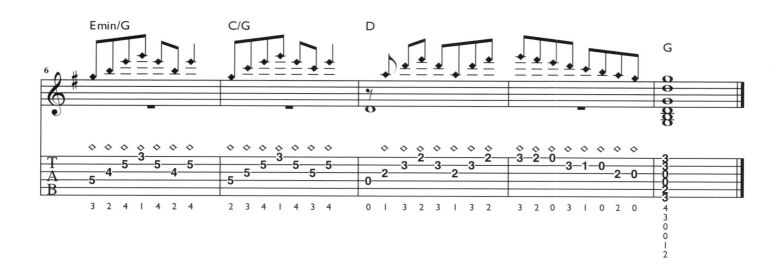

CHAPTER 8

More Theory for Arrangers

RELATIVE NATURAL MINOR

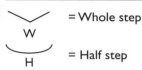

Each major scale has a *relative minor* scale. The two scales share the same notes, but start from different tonics. The relative minor is the scale built on the 6th scale degree of any major scale. It is a *natural minor* scale, which follows the step-pattern of: W–H–W–W–H–W–W.

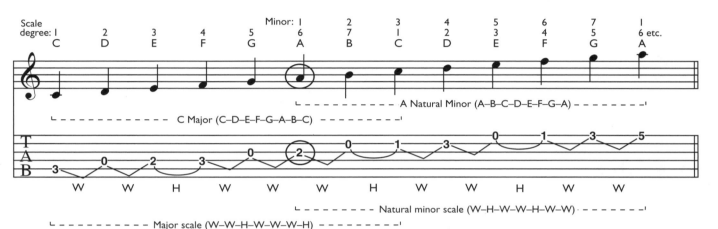

KEY SIGNATURES

Remember, a key signature (page 18) is placed after the clef on each line of music.

It indicates which notes are sharp or flat throughout a piece of music. The accidentals that appear in the key signature are those in the major scale of the same name. The quantity of sharps or flats indicates the key the music is in. A Major scale and its relative minor scale have the same key signature. Remember that the keys of C Major and A Minor have no sharps or flats.

Here are the key signatures with their corresponding major and minor keys.

SHARP KEYS

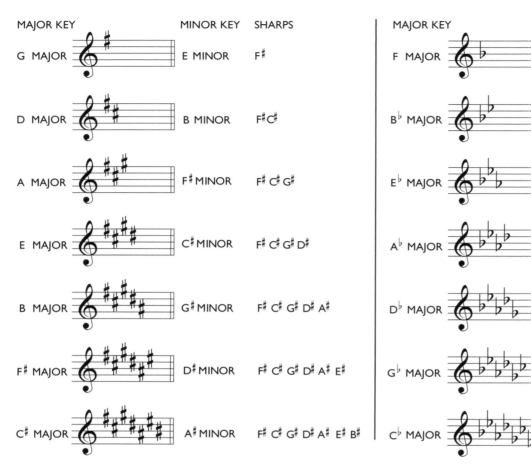

MAJOR KEY		MINOR KEY	SHARPS
G MAJOR		E MINOR	F#
D MAJOR		B MINOR	F# C#
A MAJOR		F# MINOR	F# C# G#
E MAJOR		C# MINOR	F# C# G# D#
B MAJOR		G# MINOR	F# C# G# D# A#
F# MAJOR		D# MINOR	F# C# G# D# A# E#
C# MAJOR		A# MINOR	F# C# G# D# A# E# B#

FLAT KEYS

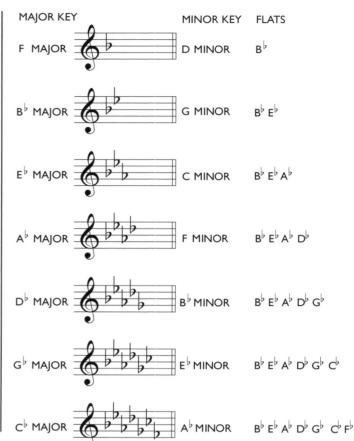

MAJOR KEY		MINOR KEY	FLATS
F MAJOR		D MINOR	B♭
B♭ MAJOR		G MINOR	B♭ E♭
E♭ MAJOR		C MINOR	B♭ E♭ A♭
A♭ MAJOR		F MINOR	B♭ E♭ A♭ D♭
D♭ MAJOR		B♭ MINOR	B♭ E♭ A♭ D♭ G♭
G♭ MAJOR		E♭ MINOR	B♭ E♭ A♭ D♭ G♭ C♭
C♭ MAJOR		A♭ MINOR	B♭ E♭ A♭ D♭ G♭ C♭ F♭

CIRCLE OF 5THS

A *circle of 5ths* depicts the major and relative minor key signatures. It is called a "circle" of 5ths because the keys are arranged *clockwise* in intervals of 5ths; 4ths are *counterclockwise*. Each time we move around the circle by a 5th, we add a sharp to that key. When we move by a 4th, we add a flat to that key. Remember, the key of C Major has no sharps or flats; it is our starting point.

In Chapter 3 (page 21), we learned how major scales are built and determined which notes are sharp or flat in every major key. The circle of 5ths delivers this same information in a way that is concise and practical.

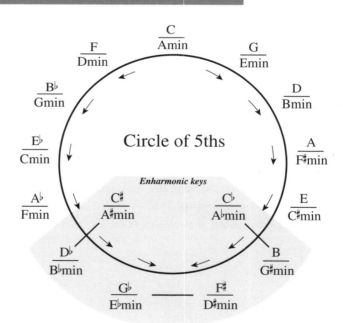

PARALLEL NATURAL MINOR SCALE

Because the major scale is the standard used to define all other harmonic concepts, it is helpful to view the natural minor scale as *parallel* to the major scale. Remember, relative keys share the same key signature, but not the same tonic (for example, A Minor and C Major). *Parallel keys* share the same tonic, but not the same key signature (for example, A Minor and A Major).

A natural minor scale can be thought of as a major scale with a $^\flat$3, $^\flat$6 and $^\flat$7.

Scale Degrees	1	2	3	4	5	6	7
A Major Scale	A	B	C$^\sharp$	D	E	F$^\sharp$	G$^\sharp$
Scale Degrees	1	2	$^\flat$3	4	5	$^\flat$6	$^\flat$7
A Natural Minor	A	B	C	D	E	F	G

DIATONIC CHORDS FOR THE NATURAL MINOR SCALE

To see which Roman numerals are used for the chords in a minor key, let's compare the chords of its parallel major key. The numerals will be the same (I–vii), but their qualities will change; as a result of this, so will the way the numeral is represented. If a major chord becomes a minor chord, it will be represented with a lower case Roman numeral (for example, I becomes i). If a minor chord becomes a major chord in the new key, it is represented with an upper case Roman numeral (for example, vi becomes VI). A flat sign $\flat$ before the III, VI and VII, indicates that those chords have been built on the lowered 3, 6 and 7 of the parallel major scale. Compare the chords of a major key to those of its parallel minor key in the chart below.

Diatonic Chords for Parallel Major and Minor Keys

Major Key	Major I	Minor ii	Minor iii	Major IV	Major V	Minor vi	Diminished vii°
Minor Key	Minor i	Diminished ii°	Major $^\flat$III	Minor iv	Minor v	Major $^\flat$VI	Major $^\flat$VII

Leo Kottke began his career on the leading edge of the fingerstyle guitar movement in the 1960s and '70s. His work—along with the work of a few others, such as John Fahey—inspired a whole new generation of fingerstyle players. Still active as a performer and recording artist, Leo Kottke's playing continues to inspire and instruct.

TRANSPOSITION

Transposition means to change the key of a piece of music. Musicians can transpose songs into keys that are suitable to their skill level. Some songs are easier to play in certain keys. We will explore this further in the next lesson.

Here are the melody and chords to "Oh, Sinner Man" in the key of D Minor.

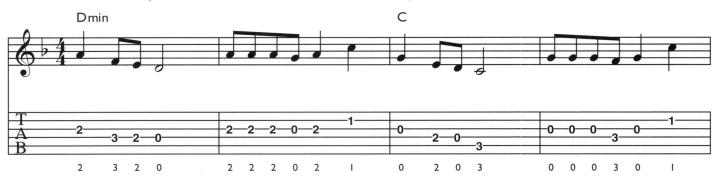

To analyze this song, let's look first at the D Natural Minor scale and its diatonic chords.

D Natural Minor	D	E	F	G	A	B♭	C
Chord Quality	min	dim	Maj	min	min	Maj	Maj
	i	ii°	♭III	iv	v	♭VI	♭VII
Scale Degree	1	2	3	4	5	6	7

There are two chords: Dmin (the i chord) and C (the ♭VII chord).

The melody starts on A (the 5 of the D Minor scale), then proceeds to F (the 3), E (the 2) and D (the 1). Continue to analyze the remainder of this melody in the following way.

Answers: bottom of page 59.

	1st Measure				2nd Measure		
Melody Notes	A	F	E	D	A	—	—	—
Scale Degree	5	3	2	1	5	—	—	—

TRANSPOSITION TO THE KEY OF A MINOR

When transposing, the *harmonic* (relating to chords) and melodic relationships must all remain intact. If a song in the key of D Minor has the i and ♭VII chords, then the song transposed to the key of A Minor must use the i and ♭VII as well. Our chords will change but their position and function within the new key will remain the same.

Here is a chart comparing the notes and chords in the keys of A Natural Minor and D Natural Minor.

Scale Degree	I	2	3	4	5	6	7
Chord Quality	min	dim	Maj	min	min	Maj	Maj
	i	ii°	♭III	iv	v	♭VI	♭VII
D Natural Minor	D	E	F	G	A	B♭	C
A Natural Minor	A	B	C	D	E	F	G

The chord progression, transposed to the key of A Minor, consists of Amin (i) and G (♭VII).

These same principals apply to the melody. Remember, our melody starts on the 5th, then proceeds to the 3rd, the 2nd, the tonic and so on. In the key of A Minor, the 5th is E, the 3rd is C, the 2nd is B, the tonic is A, and so on. Here is where your analysis of the melody in D Minor will come in handy.

Here are the chords and melody for "Oh, Sinner Man," transposed to the key of A Minor.

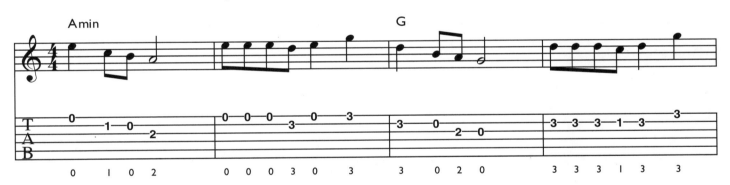

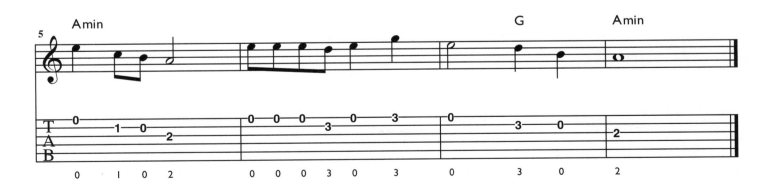

TRANSPOSITION EXERCISE

Below is a blank staff. Transpose "Oh, Sinner Man" to the key of E Natural Minor, following the process from the preceding page. Don't hesitate to make a chart comparing the keys of D Minor and E Minor; this will be very helpful at first. When you finish, check your results below.

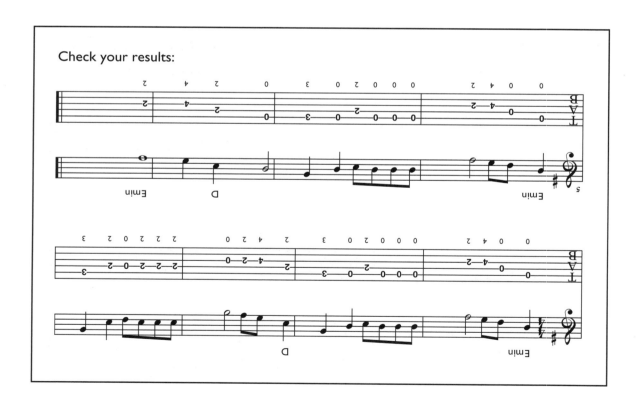

Check your results:

CHOOSING THE APPROPRIATE KEY

As mentioned earlier, some songs are easier to play in certain keys. Choosing a suitable key is critical when arranging a song to your skill-level. To do this you must first analyze the melody and harmony (chords) of your chosen song.

Considerations

- It is important to accommodate both the melody and accompaniment, with neither of them competing for notes on the fretboard.

- You must be able to play the chords in the key you are considering.

- It is best to use chords that have accessible bass notes on the bottom three strings.

- What is the range of the melody? Where are the highest and lowest notes?

- The melody and the accompaniment should be heard as separate entities within the arrangement.

- It is a good idea to keep the melody on the first three strings and the first five frets.

Let's take another look at "Oh, Sinner Man," keeping in mind the above considerations.

> **"Oh, Sinner Man" in D Minor**
> - The basic chords are Dmin and C.
> - The highest note is a C on the 2nd string; the lowest is a C on the 5th string.

The melody requires the middle four strings; it will be competing with the accompaniment for notes on the fretboard. The 1st string is not being utilized at all. For these reasons, it will be a struggle to arrange and play this song in D Minor.

> **"Oh, Sinner Man" in E Minor**
> - The basic chords are Emin and D.
> - The highest note is a D on the 2nd string; the lowest is a D on the 4th string.

The melody requires the 2nd, 3rd and 4th strings; it will be competing with the accompaniment for notes on the fretboard. The 1st string is not being utilized at all. Though this is preferable to an arrangement in D Minor, it will be challenging to arrange and play this song in E Minor.

> **"Oh, Sinner Man" in A Minor**
> - The basic chords are Amin and G.
> - The melody can be played on the first three strings.
> - The bass notes are on the lowest three strings.

A Minor seems to be the appropriate key for this song. For a confirmation of this analysis, try the arrangement of "Oh, Sinner Man" in A Minor on the next page.

Answers: page 56.

	1st Measure				2nd Measure				3rd Measure				4th Measure				5th Measure				6th Measure				7th Measure			8th
Melody Notes	A	F	E	D	A	G	A	C	G	E	D	C	G	F	G	C	A	F	E	D	A	G	A	C	A	G	E	D
Scale Degree	5	3	2	1	5	4	5	7	4	2	1	7	4	3	4	7	5	3	2	1	5	4	5	7	5	4	2	1

OH, SINNER MAN

Arrangement in A Minor

Track 38

CHAPTER 9

Advanced Arranging Tools

MELODY IN THE BASS

A common variation used when building fingerstyle arrangements is to put the melody in the lower strings and the accompaniment in the higher strings. First you must learn to play the *melody in the bass*. Here are the first four measures of "Greensleeves" in the octave it is normally played.

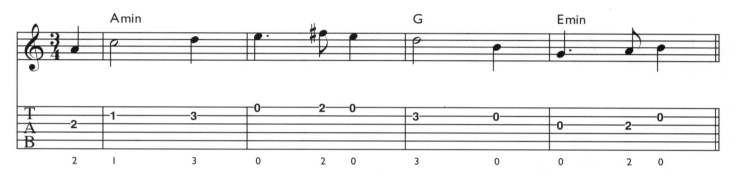

Here are the same four measures moved down one octave. Be sure to play this melody with your thumb (*p*).

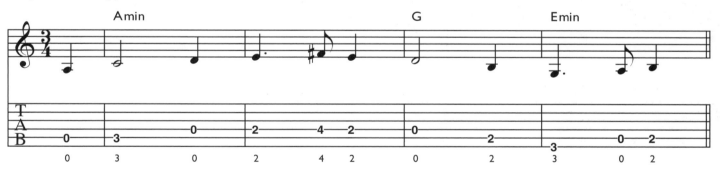

Blind Willie Johnson used this approach. Between verses of singing he would take instrumental breaks where he would play the melody on the bass strings.

Following is an arrangement of "Greensleeves" in the style of Maybelle Carter. This is often referred to as *Carter Family* style and is commonly used in country and folk. The melody is played in the bass; the chords are played when melody notes are sustained, leaving space for some accompaniment.

GREENSLEEVES

Melody in the Bass

By changing the time signature you can create a whole new feel for a piece. Here is an arrangement of "Corrinna, Corrinna," changed from $\frac{4}{4}$ to $\frac{3}{4}$. You will use a simple, palm-muted, alternating bass to accompany the melody. Once you are comfortable with the new waltz-time feel, try adding some block chords or a syncopated picking pattern.

CORRINNA, CORRINNA

Track 40

Travis Picking in $\frac{3}{4}$

Here is an arrangement of "Corrinna, Corrinna" in $\frac{6}{8}$. Remember, in this time signature, each beat is divisible into three even parts. For a review of this, see page 13 (Simple vs. Compound Meter). Tap your foot on beats 1 and 2 and count: "1–&–ah, 2–&–ah."

CORRINNA, CORRINNA
Track 41
Travis Picking in $\frac{6}{8}$

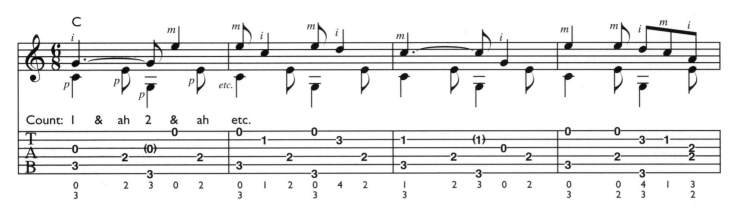

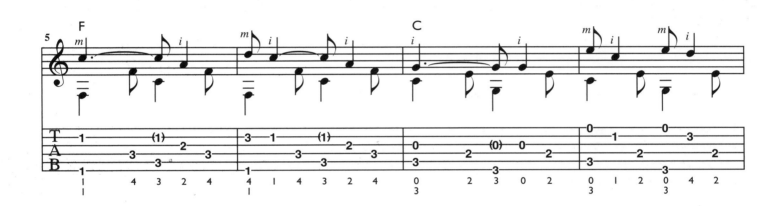

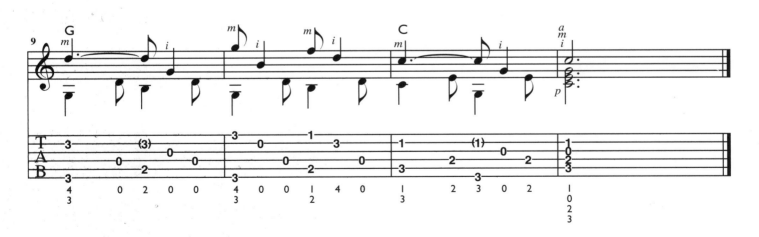

Now you have several arrangements of "Corrinna, Corrinna." Try connecting them together, making one extended arrangement. Changing from one time signature to another can take some practice—not to mention patience—so be patient. Go slow and count out loud.

Another way to create interest in an arrangement is to use chord substitutions. This involves the reharmonization of a chord progression. Substituting chords can alter the mood of a song, so let your ears be your guide.

DIATONIC SUBSTITUTIONS

Here we will look at diatonic triads (three-note chords that belong to one scale). There are three groups of chords with *common tones*. Each group is centered on one of the three major chords in the major scale. These are the primary chords (see page 23, Diatonic Harmony), which consist of the *tonic* (the I chord), the *dominant* (the V chord) and the *subdominant* (the IV chord).

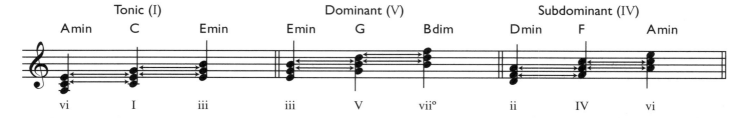

We will make substitutions from the chords within each group.

Observing the melody can also be useful when reharmonizing. For example, we can substitute an A Minor chord for a C Major chord in instances where an E- or C-note are in the melody (these are the common tones these chords share). However, if a G-note is in the melody, an E Minor chord would be a more appropriate choice because it contains the "G" not found in Amin.

Adrian Legg is not only a prominent fingerstyle guitarist, but an extraordinary storyteller and a fine photographer. Known for his remarkable technique and eclectic compositional style, he is one of today's most popular players. Check him out in the Fingerstyle Summit *with Adrian Legg, Martin Simpson and Ed Gerhard (National Guitar Workshop/Alfred-DVD #21924).*

Below is an arrangement of "A-Tisket, A-Tasket" in the key of C Major. Diatonic chord substitutions are in parentheses. Note that many of these are slash chords (see page 33).

A-TISKET, A-TASKET

Track 42

With Chord Substitutions

NON-DIATONIC SUBSTITUTIONS—SECONDARY DOMINANTS

With the exception of the tonic, the V chord, or dominant, is the strongest chord in a key. It is also the most *unstable*; it cannot stand alone, but needs to *resolve* to the I chord. Dominant chords appear most often as dominant 7 chords. Major keys and their parallel minor keys share the same dominant 7 chords.*

Here are some examples of dominant 7 chords and the I or i chords they resolve to:

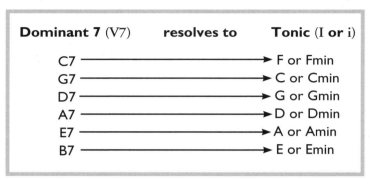

Dominant 7 (V7)	resolves to	Tonic (I or i)
C7	⟶	F or Fmin
G7	⟶	C or Cmin
D7	⟶	G or Gmin
A7	⟶	D or Dmin
E7	⟶	A or Amin
B7	⟶	E or Emin

We can utilize the strength of the dominant function by introducing *secondary dominants* into our arrangements. A secondary dominant is a dominant 7 chord that is *not* the dominant of the key you are in. It is a non-diatonic (*not* belonging to the key) chord that is built a 5th above the root of any chord in a key *besides* the tonic. It creates a stronger pull toward that chord, which, in effect, becomes a temporary tonic. The secondary dominant is the *five* of that chord. Secondary dominants are indicated with Roman numerals in this way: V/V (five of five), V/vi (five of six), etc.

Below is a common I–vi–IV–V progression. The chords in this progression are all diatonic to the key of A major. Note that the *slash notation* indicates that you can play the chords using any rhythmic or right-hand pattern you like.

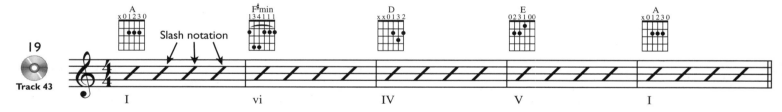

Here we have added some secondary dominants.

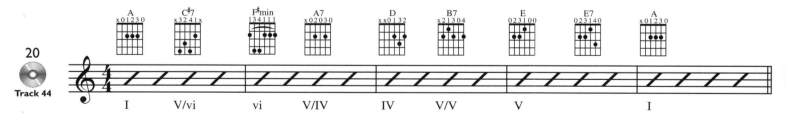

C#7 is the dominant chord of F#Minor; F#min is the vi chord of the key of A Major; therefore, C#7 is the V/vi (five of six). Continuing with this analysis, we see that A7 is the V/IV (five of four) and B7 is the V/V (five of five).

Secondary dominants are used to strengthen motion to diatonic chords. Think of secondary dominants as leverage to bend the listener's ear.

---

* A true minor key is harmonized with the notes of the *harmonic minor scale*, which is a natural minor scale with a ♭7. This transforms the dominant chord from a minor to a major triad or dominant 7 and provides a stronger pull back to the tonic.

Here is an arrangement of "Billy the Kid" with diatonic substitutions and secondary dominants.

 **BILLY THE KID**

Track 45

CHAPTER 10

Alternate Tunings

An alternate tuning is any tuning other than standard tuning (E–A–D–G–B–E).

DROP D TUNING: D–A–D–G–B–E

For *drop D tuning,* you must "drop," or tune down, your 6th string one whole step from E to D. It is usually indicated with: ⑥=D

Track 46

You can tune to the CD for this book. There are also several ways you can tune to drop D yourself.

1. Use an electronic tuner.

2. Match the 7th fret of the 6th string to the open 5th string.

3. Match the harmonic on the 12th fret of the 6th string to the open 4th string.

4. Match the 6th string to one octave below the 4th string.

This tuning allows you to maintain an alternating bass, while playing chords from either D Major or D Minor higher up the neck on the first three strings. Check this out.

TICKETY-BOO TOOD

Track 47
Drop D Tuning

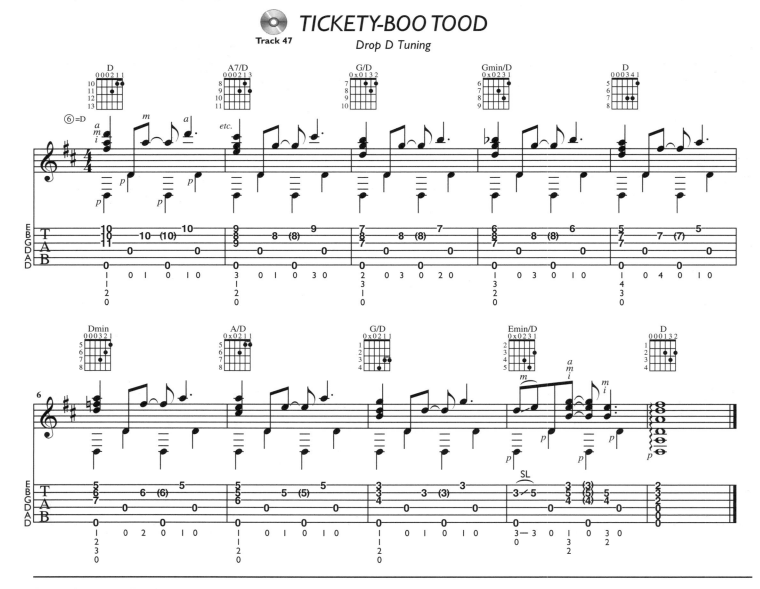

Here's an arrangement of "Camptown Races" in drop D, utilizing the length of the fretboard. Try palm muting throughout.

CAMPTOWN RACES

Track 48

Drop D Tuning

One of the most common alternate tunings is *open G tuning*. In an *open tuning,* the open strings form a chord; in this case, a G chord. Many players, including Joni Mitchell, Leo Kottke and Robert Johnson, have used this tuning regularly.

From standard tuning, drop your 6th, 5th and 1st strings down one whole step (6th and 1st strings—E down to D; 5th string—A down to G). The 4th, 3rd and 2nd strings remain as they are (D–G–B).

Track 49

You can tune to the CD for this book. Here are two other options:

1. Use an electronic tuner.

2. Match octaves: The 1st string should be lowered to one octave above the 4th string (D), the 6th string should be lowered to one octave below the 4th string (D) and the 5th string should be lowered to one octave below the 3rd string (G). Your ear may not be capable of matching octaves at first, but after you have used the electronic tuner awhile, you will get used to how the strings are supposed to sound. The ear is a muscle that needs to be "worked out" for it to develop.

Here are some common chord shapes you will find helpful when arranging songs in this tuning.

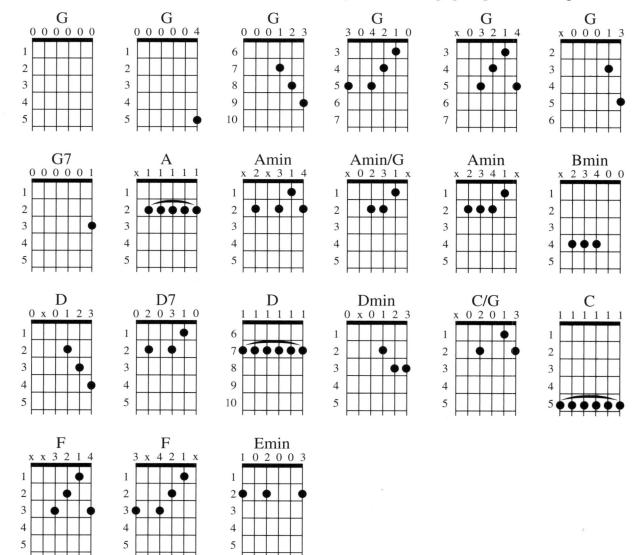

Here is a G Major scale in the first position and up the 1st string in open G tuning.

G Major Scale (Open G Tuning)

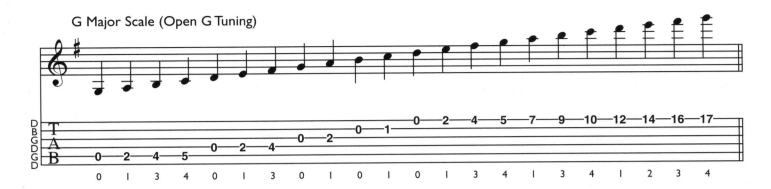

Below are the diatonic 6ths (on the 4th and 2nd strings) of the G Major scale in open G tuning. Remember, these intervals are commonly used to harmonize melodies.

Diatonic 6ths of the G Major Scale (Open G Tuning)

Mississippi John Hurt began playing guitar in 1903. A farm laborer, he developed his unique fingerpicking style in obscurity. It wasn't until the folk revival of the 1950s and 1960s that he received recognition by a mass audience. Suddenly, he found himself making more money than he ever thought possible. Until months before his death, he continued to record and perform as an artist who was in his prime.

Here is your first song in open G tuning. Notice that most of the melody is harmonized in 3rds and 6ths. In measures 17–24, triplets are played over a monotonic bass. The first note of each triplet is a note of the melody.

YANKEE DOODLE

Open G Tuning

* These are not slurred slides. Pluck all of the notes.

Open D tuning is another common alternate tuning. From standard tuning, drop the 6th and 1st strings one whole step from E to D. Then drop the 2nd string one whole step from B to A. Now drop the 3rd string a half step from G to F♯.

Track 51

You can tune to the CD for this book. Other tuning options are:

1. Use an electronic tuner.

2. Match octaves: The 1st string (E) should be lowered to one octave above the 4th string (D). The 6th string (E) should be lowered to one octave below the 4th string (D) and the 2nd string (B) should be lowered to one octave above the 5th string (A). Match the 3rd string open to the 4th string, 4th fret.

Here are some common chord shapes used in this tuning.

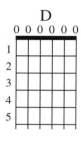 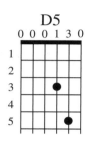 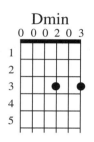 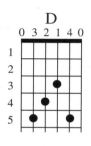 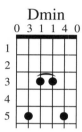

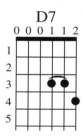 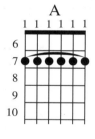 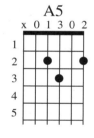 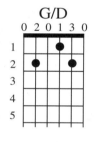 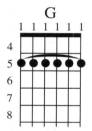

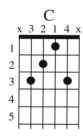 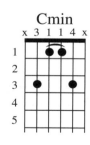 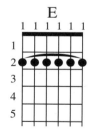 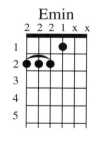 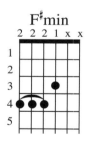

The traditional song, "Jesus On the Mainline," has been done by both Joseph Spence and Ry Cooder. Here it is arranged for open D tuning.

JESUS ON THE MAINLINE

Track 52

Open D Tuning

Here's another favorite in open D tuning.

AMAZING GRACE
Track 53

Open D Tuning

CHAPTER 11

Cross-String Technique

The technique of *cross-string* playing (sometimes called *harp-style* playing) can be heard in the playing of Pierre Bensusan and Seth Austen. The objective is to produce a harp-like effect. This is another great way to achieve legato (smooth, connected) *phrases* (short musical ideas) as discussed on page 42.

Below are two musical examples. Notice that the notes in standard notation, in both examples, are the same. However, the fingerings as indicated in the TAB, are different. Example 22 is accomplished with cross-string playing. These examples are in standard tuning.

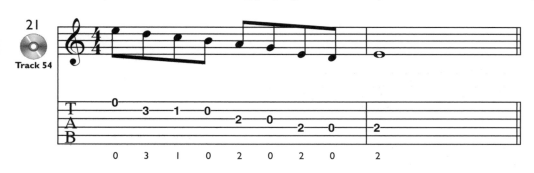

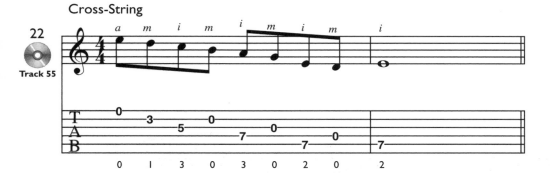

Observe the first three notes in the examples above. In example 21, to play the C-note, you must lift your 3rd finger from the D-note on the 3rd fret. In example 22, all three notes are fingered simultaneously. This concept continues throughout the example.

To accomplish this technique, it is necessary to relocate some lower notes further up the neck on lower strings. Try to arrange phrases so that each note has its own string and is held as long as possible.

To get the full effect of harp-style playing, hold the notes down as long as you can. This creates more sustain, which is desirable when going for a legato sound.

Below are some more cross-string examples. Once you get your fingers around these, you're
ready to try the arrangement of "Li'l Liza Jane" on the next page. Remember to observe the
fingering in the TAB.

23
Track 56

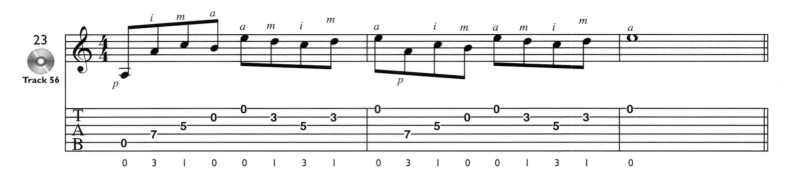

24
Track 57

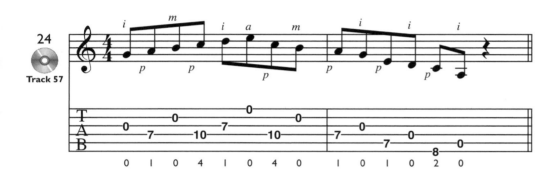

25
Track 58

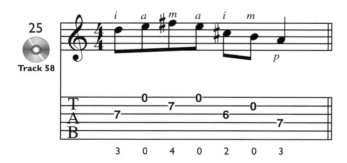

26
Track 59

LI'L LIZA JANE

Cross-String Arrangement

ARRANGEMENTS

ARRANGEMENT I—ARRANGEMENT BLUES

Here is a *24-bar blues,* which follows the same form as the 12-bar blues, but each measure is played twice as long. This song uses a monotonic bass (page 17) in the style of blues legend, Lightnin' Hopkins. The melody, however, is more quirky than bluesy. Slurs are prevalent in this arrangement.

Practice tips

1. The cross-string *lick* (short melodic phrase) in bars 3 and 4 is repeated in bars 23 and 24.

2. The natural harmonic (page 46) in bar 12 should be played with the 3rd finger of your left hand.

ARRANGEMENT BLUES
Track 61

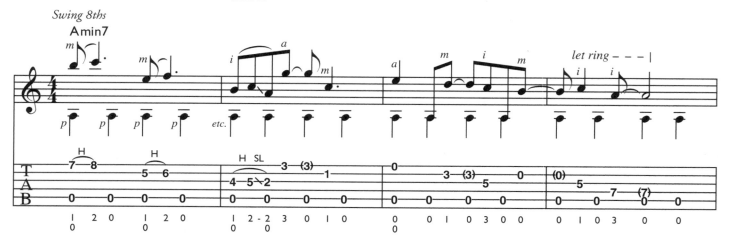

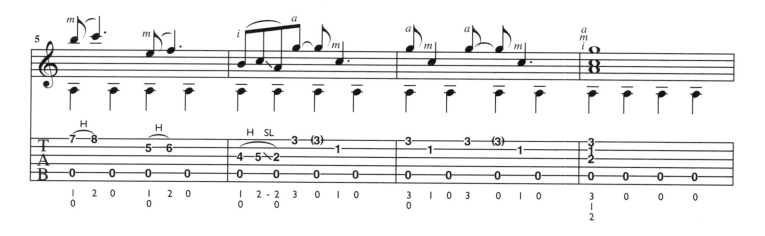

This piece features an alternating bass, hammer-ons and a syncopated picking pattern; it is essential for the beginning fingerstyle guitarist to develop these techniques. This arrangement is reminiscent of the style of Bruce Cockburn, in whose playing the influence of Mississippi John Hurt is apparent.

BIG YELLOW LUNCH BOX
Track 62

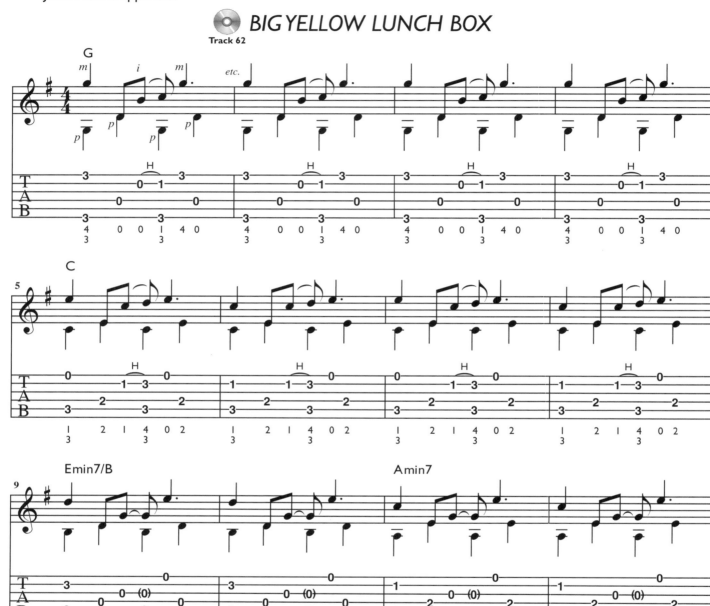

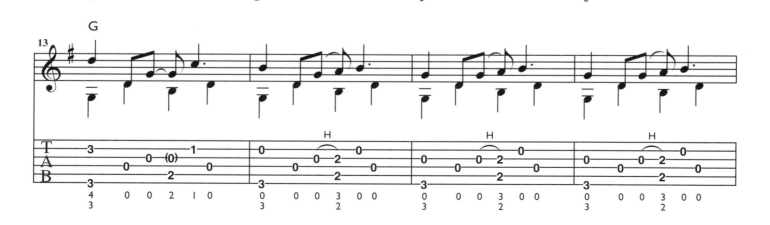

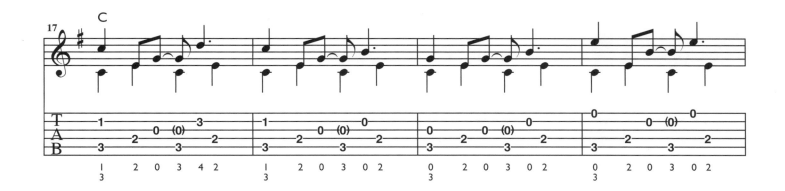

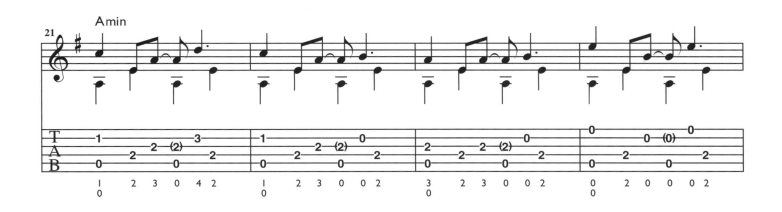

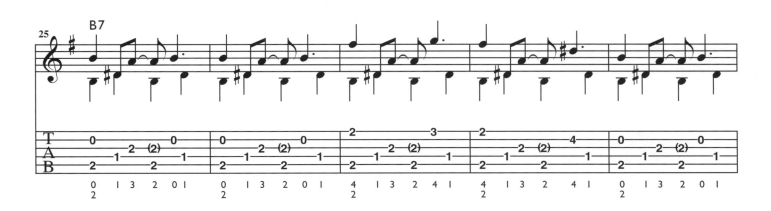

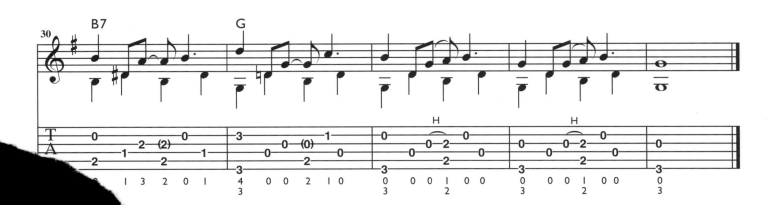

The next arrangement is another 24-bar blues. It's in the key of D Major and uses drop D tuning. Below are the chord shapes you will use to play this arrangement. Hollow dots indicate melody notes played while holding the chord. The left-hand fingers used to fret these notes are inside the hollow dots.

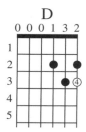

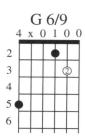

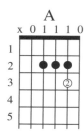

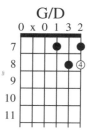

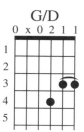

Practice tips

Part A (measures 1–24) uses an alternating bass with a syncopated picking pattern.

Part B (measures 25–48) is in the style of blues artist, Taj Mahal. Here we maintain the alternating bass and play slurred notes around the *5th position* D Major chord (*position* indicates where the 1st finger is located—in this case, the 5th fret). Note that the natural harmonic found in measure 28 should be played with the 3rd finger of your left hand.

Part C (measures 49–76) departs from the blues form. In measures 49–56, we move further up the neck to develop the sliding *motif* (short melodic or rhythmic figure that appears throughout a song) introduced in part B. Measures 57–69 are in the style of eclectic blues artist, Chris Smither. We descend from the 9th to the 2nd position using triad chord shapes found on the first three strings. This is accomplished while maintaining the alternating bass. Notice the *train lick* (short for "Freight Train" lick, which involves upward motion from a minor 3rd to a major 3rd) in measures 61–63. This is another sound common to Smither's playing. Measures 69–76 are in the style of Mississippi John Hurt's "Coffee Blues." Here we are using the F♮- and F♯-notes to create a bluesy sound with the D chord; this is similar to the train lick of measures 61–63.

Song Form: Play until you get to the direction, *D.C. al Coda,* which is short for *Da Capo al Coda. Capo* means "head," or beginning. *D.C. al Coda* tells you to repeat from the beginning until you see *To Coda* ⊕, then skip to the *Coda* (the ending of a piece of music). In other words, play measures 1–76; then repeat measures 1–48; then jump to measure 77 and play to the end.